HUMAN RIGHTS AND DEVELOPMENT:
Issue and Challenges

Human Rights and Development:
Issue and Challenges

Jagat Pal

SERIALS PUBLICATIONS
NEW DELHI (INDIA)

First Published - 2010

ISBN: 978-81-8387-423-6

Published by

SERIALS PUBLICATIONS
4830/24, Prahlad Street, Ansari Road
Darya Ganj, New Delhi-110002 (India)
Phone : 23245225 Fax : 91-11-23272135
E-mail: serials@sify.com

Contents

Preface

Indian Education System is a well established education system in the world. There are more than 300 universities in India which are imparting education in various disciplines. These universities are Academic Universities, Medical Universities, Agricultural Universities, high level engineering institutions, Indian Institutes of Technology, Indian Institutes of Managements, polytechnics, and law institutions and colleges of law. Starting from the ancient times with the establishment of Nalanda, the biggest Buddhist University in Asia and Taxila University, India has been the Centre of high level of education where foreign students were also studying. The Indian Universities pass out several thousands student in various disciplines every year.

Law Education now a days occupy a very substantial and important place in the university curriculum and every university has a Faculty of Law in it to impart law education to its students. The universities are being assisted by law colleges and law schools which are affiliated to the university. Still further, the law education is being imparted through distance education and enabling students who are unable to attend the whole time law courses. Law like other disciplines occupy an important place in the University Grants Commission's educational business. Law education owes its existence to the overbearing needs of all social, economic, political and humanitarian considerations experienced by huma civilization.

Legal education was recognized by Lord Cornwallis in 1 during British regime. Gradually it developed in diff universities of India with different syllabi. After indepe Parliament by enacting Advocate Act, 1961, has given a to Bar Council of India on legal education.

This volume include nine research articles by law experts and holding supreme positions in seats of learning in India and abroad. However these articles comprehensively and systematically educate the researchers and law students in legality of human rights, natural rights and others rights which are fundamental to human beings viz Fundamental Rights. These research articles educate all in the law and its application in all the spheres- social, economic, political, religious, cultural rights and enlightens them to legal aspects of Right to Live, Right to Livelihood, right to medical assistance, Rights to Freedom of Speech, Right to Religion, Right to Occupation and so on. In fact the objectives and main purpose of these articles is to educate the mind on legal consideration and application of law on various sphere of life which indirectly affect individual life.

The article 'Idea of Right" educates us what the rights are, and what is their legal application, how a person lay claim on certain legal, cultural, political, religious, property, education, and conventional rights. These are not natural rights. The study reveals what is the basic origin of rights and they came to various different forms. The article cites various practical examples to support the view of rights and their legality.

The article 'Urban Development and Indian Judiciary: Panorama of a New Environmental Jurisprudence' The reader has an opportunity to peen into the working of the Indian Judiciary through judgments delivered by apex court on various cases. The article is a very comprehensive article on Indian Judiciary which goes a long way to understand the law education in the right direction with practical view. The study has tried to assess various ...nent of the Apex Court and different high courts delivered ... to time so as to trace the development of the thought ... Indian Judiciary has also been influenced by the ...ch of development in delivering their judgments. ...arious laws and articles in delivery of judgment ...al aspect of education. The study also deals ...risprudence and judgments delivered on ...ronment, its protection, preservation, and ...e studies are landmark of judgment on ...ence. A law student will derive the ...valuable judgment which can help in ... aspect of study on environment. The article traced complete history of environmental jurisprudence till to date and post-1990 development in the field of environmental management. Indian Judiciary by adopting, applying and transforming these doctrines into an integral part of Indian Law has shown the path to perceive development in inclusive sense of improvement of linking all aspects of human welfare been natural social, economic and political in a given society.

The article 'Right to Medical Assistance and Constitution of India' by Ganeshji Tiwari and Sanjay Kumar Singh, is not only a detailed study of provisions provide information in the Constitution of India for Right to Medical Assistance but is a very practical and interesting study of the subject. An effort has been made to educate all in the direction of health care as per constitutional study. It imparts practical legal education to a common man and a law researcher that how a person has a right to medical assistance. The article legally studies the position with legal court judgments. A person who meets accident and is brought to hospital for medical treatment but denied the same due to non-completion of formalities of police etc. Under the provisions of constitution the patient cannot be denied the treatment for non-completion of formalities. It is a very learned study of Right to Health at various stages of Life. Right to health and medical care to protect health and vigour, while in service and after retirement was held as a Fundamental Right of a worker under Article 21 of Constitution of India. Various judgments have been cited delivered by High Courts and Supreme Court issues related to the Health, medical assistance. Right to life and Personal liberty includes Right to Health and medical assistance. It also educate on legality of Right to Privacy, while enriching one's legal knowledge on health and medical assistance one can also enrich his legal application of various laws.

The volume includes other equally important and information rich articles as detailed below:

Socio-Economic Care and Human Rights: Unfolding the myth, Virtues, Perfectionism and Natural Law, Human Rights and Development: an analysis with special Concern to Environment, Funding Footing in a post-Modern conception of Law, Formalism or Pragmatism, the Myth and Reality of Legal Education in India.

The last article 'The Myth and Reality of Legal Education in India' by RP Upadhayaya is brief description but compact and information full, and maps the legal education in India, describes the aims and objectives of legal education, how Lord Denning defined the legal education's aims. Comprehensively deals with historical development of legal education in India, law courses, UGC, Bar Council of India, Legal Committees etc. It also enunciates idea of National law Schools as autonomous universities under respective State Statutes and suggest means and measures on improving quality of legal education and resolving the problems in the legal educational system.

In view of the above, the volume proves its worth as a educating tool of legal education in India with very critical studies of judgments delivered on various aspects of law and various articles and at the same time their application. Therefore it will prove a very useful study material on legal education in India. Such books are asset to the rich collection of various libraries and information centres in the country. It contains rare material of the subject which is very helpful for research and studentship.

The Idea of Right

Jagat Pal*

What does it mean to have a right? If to have a right means to have a certain justified claim to a certain kind of positive and negative treatment from others, then right exists between the right-holders and others. The righi-holders and others who have the capacity for discharging duties correlated to a right of the right holders constitute the terms of a relation of right. If this be so, then the field of a relation of right would be the totality of all those who have the capacities for discharging duties correlative to a right of the right-holders and that of all those who hold that right. For example, if x has right to life, then y has a certain kind of positive and negative duties to x. The negative duties correlated to the right to life of x consist in not interfering in the life of x, i.e., not harming, not killing or causing injury to x. If y harms, kills or causes injury to the life of x, y breaches his duty to x. The positive duties correlated to the right to life of x consist in helping or assisting x in preservation of his right to life. If y does not help or assist x by doing the duties correlative to the right to life of x, y breaches his duty to x. The reason is that because the right to life of x always requires a certain kind of positive and negative treatments from y, the moment when y sincerely accepts that x has the right to life. This is analytically true in the light of the very definition of the notion of 'right' itself. The right to life is a justified claim which x makes against y. If y does not do his positive and negative duties correlated to the right to life of x or acts contrary to it, x has the privilege to act the way x thinks deems to be fit rationally under the situation to preserve his

* *Department of Philosophy, North Eastern Hill University, Shillong-793022*

right to life, and y has no right to say that x not to act that way. If y attacks x, x has the privilege to use force in his defense. This privilege y cannot say that x does not have. If we accept this view of right, then it implies that the right-holder has autonomy to decide whether or not to hold one's right. The idea of autonomy is inbuilt in the idea of right. If this be so, then x also has the privilege to use force in his defense when y attacks on him and y has no right to say that x not to act that way.

But then it can be held by someone against someone else only when the right-holders and others against whom the claim of right is made possess a certain kind of mental maturity for to have social interaction. A being that has no sense of right cannot make the claim of right against other. So also is the case vice versa. If others with whom the right-holders cannot communicate their claim of right possessed by them and they have no capacity for discharging duties correlated to a right of the right-holders, the right-holders cannot make their claim of right against them. If so, then from this it is quite clear that the claim of right cannot be made by an infant, an idiot and a mad person against others because to make a claim against someone else always requires a certain kind of mental maturity which infants, idiots and mad persons do not possess in them in the actuality. To enter into a relation of right is, thus, to participate in a social transaction and that is possible only between such beings with whom one can communicate one's right and the communicated being also understands that claim of right made against him. So, if we define 'right' as a justified claim by someone against someone else, it logically assumes that the individuals who enter into a relation of right are full-fledged maturated human individuals with whom one can have social interaction. This means that the field of a relation of right consists of only matured human beings.

It is quite possible that the idea of right may involve in it a cluster of rights. Take, for example, the idea of right to life. The idea of right to life is such that it involves in it a cluster of rights, i.e., the right not to be harmed, the right not to be killed, the right not to be injured, the right not to be attacked, the right to self-dignity, the right to self-respect, the right to self-defense, etc. So, if y sincerely accepts that x has the right to life, then y cannot say that he has no positive and negative duties correlated to a cluster of rights involved in the idea of right to life of x. If y says that he sincerely accepts that x has the right to life but has no positive and negative duties correlated to a cluster of rights involved in the idea of right to life of x, it would amount to mean that y does not understand meaning of the word 'right'. He misuses the word 'right'. The word 'right' is a value word. It is not a descriptive word. It involves prescriptive element in it. If y still insists that he sincerely accepts that x has the right to life but cannot do his duties correlated to a cluster of rights involved in the idea of right to life of x under a particular situation, then y is required to give good reasons to justify his statement. If y says that he sincerely accepts that x has the right to life but does not give good reasons for his not doing duties correlated to the right to life of x under a particular situation, it would amount to mean that y does not sincerely accept that x has the right to life. In other words, y cannot assent to x has the right to life and dissent from a cluster of duties correlated to it unless there are good reasons. If this is so, then to say x has the right to life means to say x has the right to life against y, and y has a certain kind of obligations to x. And to say this means to say that x and y belong to the domain of a relation of right in a social context. The idea of right acquires its meaning only in social interaction of one to other. So, if the right to life is a justified claim which x makes against y, then y cannot be an infant, an idiot, a mad person or a non-human being because such beings have no mental and physical abilities which being dutiful to x always requires. He has to be an adult normal human being with whom x can communicate his claim of right to life meaningfully, the one who has mental capacity to understand that claim and also does have the physical ability for discharging duties correlated to the right to life of x. If y does not have the capacity for discharging duties correlated to the right to life of x which being dutiful always requires, x cannot make his claim of right to life against y even if y belongs to the human species and has the potentiality to grow into an adult normal human individual, a full fledged member with whom x can have social interaction in future. Not only this, x also cannot make his claim of right to life against y if y has no freedom for discharging duties correlated to it. If x himself does not have a certain kind of mental maturity, x also cannot make his claim of right to life against y even if x has the potentiality for making that claim in future because to make the claim of right by someone against someone else always requires the actual and not the potential mental capacity. If so, then x and y can enter into a relation of right in a social world only when they themselves possess a certain level of mental maturity and also do have some idea of right. The idea of right has no meaning outside the domain of a social world because it can be claimed by someone against someone else meaningfully only within a social world.

The idea of right is such that duties correlated to it may hold to oneself as well as someone else. Take, for example, the idea of right to life. If x has the right to life and also has the capacity which being dutiful requires, then the right to life of x not only binds y not to harm or to kill x. It also binds x not to harm or to kill himself. If x harms or kills himself, he acts contrary to his right to life. The idea of right to life abnegates the destruction of life. But then the duties correlated to the right to life binds to oneself only when the right-holders are adult normal human beings, the beings who have the capacity for discharging duties correlated to it to oneself. It does not bind on those who are not adult normal human beings. Above all, to say that the right to life of x binds y to do a certain kind of positive and negative duties correlated to it is not to say that y cannot have that right, and x cannot have those positive and negative duties correlated to the right to life towards y. If both x and y have the right to life and also do have the capacities for discharging duties correlated to the right to life, they cannot escape from the obligations correlated to the right to life against one another and also to oneself. But such a relation of right can be held by someone to oneself or to other only when they have the power of agency. It cannot be held by such beings that have no power of agency which being dutiful always requires. When a relation of right exists between adult normal human beings reciprocatively, the right of one imposes a certain kind of duties on the other. So, if 'right' is defined as justified claim by someone against someone else, then it can exist between adult normal human beings only, i.e., the persons who possess the feature of agency in the actuality. There are no rights without duty. The idea of agency is central to the idea of right and the idea of agency logically rests on the idea of the autonomy of an agent which consists in deliberative, decision-making, ability and doing action freely as and when the occasion demands on him.

But sometimes we do not shape our conception of right in this sense. We shape our conception of right by dissociating the idea of agency from it. We associate our idea of right with the idea of interest. And when we associate our idea of right with the idea of interest, we say any entity that has interest has right. It is based on this premise we quite often argue that one can have rights without any duty. Take, for example, fetuses, infants, children, idiots, mad persons. We do say that fetuses, infants, children and mad persons have rights on us, but have no duties towards us. When we say this, we say simply on this ground because we believe that they also do have interests like us to grow into a full-fledged individual. And in saying it, we never associate the idea of right with the idea of agency; we associate the idea of right with the idea of interest. Since fetuses, infants, children and mad persons have interests; they have rights on us but have no duties towards us. They have no duties towards us simply because they lack the power of agency in the actuality which being dutiful always requires. To say this does not mean to say that they lack the power of agency in the potentiality. These human beings do have the power of agency in the potentiality. But we do not shape our conception of duty on it. We shape our conception of duty on the actual power of agency. A mother cannot deny that it is her duty to feed her child. The child has right on the mother to be fed. The mother cannot say that the child has the duty not to cry or disturb her. She also cannot deny that the child has right to be fed. If so, then someone's having a right on someone else does not always bind on the former owing a duty to the latter, nor does someone's having a duty towards someone else always bind on the former having a right on the latter. The mother has duty to feed the child, but have no right to be fed by the child. The relation of being dutiful towards the child is possible not on this ground because the child has the potentiality being dutiful towards us but on this ground because the child has interest like us to grow into a full-fledged normal individual human being. What is true of the fetuses, infants, children and mad persons also is true of the animals and other living beings as well because they also do have interests to grow into a full-fledged individual organism and this interest is a natural one. We cannot say that fetuses, infants, children and mad persons have rights on us on this ground because they have interests like us but animals have no rights on us even though they have interests. If we say this, it would amount to mean making a self-contradictory statement. The animals also have rights on us not to be killed or tortured, but have no duties towards us because they also have interests like us to grow into a full-fledged individual organism. The relation of being dutiful to animals is perfectly possible even if animals have no sense of right because holding a right does not necessitate having a sense of right. A being can have right even if it has no sense of right. Being dutiful to any being also does not necessitate that being must have a sense of right. A person can be dutiful to any being even if that being has no sense of right. If so, then fetuses, infants, children, mad persons and animals, etc., can have rights on us even if they have no sense of right or duties towards us. A relation of right can exist between human beings, irrespective of whether or not they have the power of agency in the actuality. It can also exist between human and non-humans, irrespective of whether or not they have the power of agency in the potentiality. The reason is that because the idea of right does not logically rest on the idea of the knowledge of right, nor does it logically rest on the idea of duty which requires the power of agency. Therefore, we cannot say that fetuses, infants, children and mad persons have rights on us but animals have no rights on us. Because what constitutes as a ground to say that fetuses, infants, children and mad persons have rights on us also constitutes as a ground to say that animals have rights on us. To deny this would to mean making a self contradictory statement and to make a self-contradictory statement means to commit the fallacy of inconsistency. So, if we shape our conception of right by associating it with the idea of interest and not with the idea of agency, we can say very well that animals have rights on us but have no duties towards us because to attribute right is not to attribute duty and to attribute duty is not to attribute right.

The idea of right does not in itself possess natural or moral or legal or cultural or religious or economic or social or political meaning. It all depends upon its use. When we derive rights from the laws of nature, we call them as natural rights. When we derive rights from the laws of morals, we call them as moral rights. When derive rights from the legal laws, we call them as legal rights. When we talk about human beings that they possess a certain kinds of right by virtue of their rational nature of human being, we use the word 'right' in a natural sense. These rights are believed to be essential for all human beings, irrespective of their caste, creed, colour, gender and culture, etc. We all need them in order to grow into a full-fledged individual human being. These rights are also called birth rights. They are the right to life, the right to freedom, the right to self-dignity, the right to choose, the right to decide, the right to defense, etc. These rights do not gain their force through legislation. Legal rights, cultural rights, political rights, economic rights, religious rights, property rights, educational rights are called as conventional rights. They not called as natural rights. These rights are called as conventional rights because they derived from the rules of convention of a particular society. Take, for example, the legal rights. The legal rights are not derived from the laws of nature. They are derived from the legal laws of a society and the legal laws of a society are human made laws. They gain their force through legislation. We justify them by referring to the existing system of the laws of a society. These rights are not universal rights because the laws from which they are derived are not universal laws like the natural laws. The legal laws differ from society to society, time to time and situation to situation. What is true of the legal rights is also true of the economic rights, political rights, religious rights, cultural rights and educational rights as well. All these rights are owned by conventions. They not universal rights owned by all human beings by virtue of their nature of being a human. The conventional rights are specific rights which human beings enjoy by virtue of their being a member of the conventional system of a society. But to say this does not mean that rights are always held by individuals only. Rights can be held by groups also because there is nothing in the idea of right that prevents groups from having it.

Thus, what sorts of entities have rights and what sorts of entities have no rights depends upon our views and interpretations on it; and our views and interpretations on it do differ. Some people derive rights from the rational feature of human beings, i.e., rationalists. So, when they talk about rights, they think about human beings only because it is they according to them who possess the feature of rationality and none else. But some people derive rights from the divinity, i.e., theologians. According to them, rights are accorded by the divine being, that is, God. So, when they talk about rights, they think about both human and non-human entities. Some people derive rights from the natural interest that a being and species possess, i.e., environmentalists. According to them, all human and non-human entities including their species have rights on us because they have some natural interests like us to grow and reproduce. So, when they talk about rights, they think not only about individual human and non-human entities but also their species and eco-systems. Some people even talk about rights of those entities which are yet to be born, i.e., future generations. According to them, we all owe certain duties to posterity and posterity has some rights on us. This means that the limit on what sorts of entities have rights and what sorts of entities have no rights logically depend upon our conception of right which we entertain about them and our views and interpretations on it are bound to be different. But this is not a peculiar characteristic of the value word 'right' only. It is the general characteristic of all the value words.

Urban Development and Indian Judiciary: Panorama of a New Environmental Jurisprudence

RANJIT SIL*

AMONG the challenges of 21st Century World urban renewal and city development is the greatest one with the allied problems like uncontrolled deforestation, unplanned human settlement, congested urban agglomerates, watershed degradation, greenhouse effect etc. Generally, the developed nations are in the terminal stage of urbanization while developing ones are in acceleration stage. Industrialization in developing countries has led the urbanization process in an unplanned and haphazard manner at the cost of ecological consideration. In the context the present concept of 'human ecology' is emphasizing on the need of recognizing ecological considerations in the formulation of developmental plans of the countries like India. Local approaches to urban development are mainly responsible for creating environmental crisis. The conventional approaches have failed to maintain ecological sustainability. New direction in analyzing environmental and resource problems has pushed forward the development of an emerging economics of sustainable development. Therefore, an alternative approaches to development as the most recent theory of development is looked into by different branches of study. The Indian Judiciary, of late, has come across with very complex eco problems while dealing with different developmental issues which came up before it for the judgment. The courts have been confronted

* *Assistant Professor, Department of Law and Legal Jurisprudence Studies, Sikkim University.*

with problems of different multitude as to issues of resource conservation, environmental management, deforestation, environmental degradation, unaccountable administration affected by uncontrolled developmental activities. The judicial policing being guided by the general constitutional provisions and some other micro provisions and enactments dealing with the areas of 'human settlement' and 'environment' has opened a new environmental jurisprudence to address the goal of human dignity and to save the earth from unchecked degradation.

In the light of the above observation the paper has tried to assess various judgments of the Apex Court and different High Courts delivered from time to time so as to trace the development of the thought that how the Indian Judiciary has also been influenced by the alternative approach of development in delivering their judgment. The pre 1990 judicial decisions had already started interpreting right to life as inclusive of right to clean environment. But the post 1990 judicial decisions have set in a remarkable trend of establishing an alternative approach of Indian developmental model based on relation between man and nature, development not in isolation from environment and gave rise to a number of Doctrines like Sustainable Development, Precautionary Principle, Principle of Intergenerational Equity etc. and thereby has transformed the doctrine into a legal obligation and constitutional mandate for the government.

Development is fundamentally an economic process and basically meant for improving the conditions of life. In capitalist modernity progress is conventionally understood as economic growth. As per Marxism's thesis capitalism is a class in which minority owns and controls the means of the production and thereby, determine the character and direction of development, the social relations with nature. Production is organized not as a social activity that directly satisfies need, but as a profit making endeavour in which needs are met only when profit can be made. Therefore, in capitalist modernity economic growth becomes a necessity rather than a choice in which consumption occurs in ignorance of its long run environmental and social consequences.

The spirit of the constitution of India is to establish a rule of the law society wherein the concept of social justice is enshrined following the philosophy of egalitarian society and Gandhi's

Daridra Narain. Article 21 of the constitution of India guarantees the fundamental right to life to all the people of India and the Supreme Court of India has interpreted that right to life includes the right to have a living environment as inherent in the right to life congenial to human existence. To realize this right the state has been directed to endeavour to protect and improve the environment and safeguard the forests and wildlife of the country.[1] The Supreme Court assumed the role of savour of the masses from environmental pollution and opened a new vista for the general public to approach the court immediately through public interest litigation.[2] The year 1986 is a new trend setter in the history of the human settlement issues when the Supreme Court in case of *Surat Municipality Corporation vs Ramesh Chandra*[3] delivered an important judgment by declining to evict persons from their hutments observing that the right to hutment dwellers to stay and to have roofs over their heads is their fundamental right as included in right to life, a constitutional guarantee and thereby did a social engineering bringing a balance between the right to existence of the vast majority of the poor people who are the real source of power in a democratic society in one hand and the profit and comfort of the few individuals, on the other hand. The fact of the case was that the owner of a plot, in order to develop it and thereby to get optimum return of the investment made by him, filed a case against the municipal corporation to remove the hutment dwellers those were living on the three sides of the said plot for the last ten years.

In K. Ramdas Shenoy vs The Chief Officer, Town Municipal Council, Udipi[4], a landmark Supreme Court Zoning Case in the early 70's where the responsible municipal authorities violated a town planning scheme by authorizing a cinema building in a residential area and the court was not at all impressed by the argument that the illegal construction should be allowed because the respondent had spent money, the Supreme Court observed that the violation of environment cannot continue and upsetting an ecological balance will be judged with even more strict standards.[5]

. Under the common law the ownership denotes the right of the owner to possess, use and enjoy the thing he owns, even to consume, destroy or alienate the thing owned. But this concept of individual ownership is in contrast with the communal enjoyment of individual property. The Court examined the matter from the view of our legal and Constitutional obligation to preserve and protect our ecology and environment. *T. Damodhar Rao vs Hyderabad (Special Officer, Municipal Corporation of Hyderabad)*[6] reflected the judicial view of collectivist jurisprudence of municipal administration which has substantially curtailed the common law doctrine of private ownership, clearing its vision that protection of environment is not only the duty of the citizen but it is also the obligation of the state and all other state organs including courts.[7]

A great American judge, emphasizing the imperative issue of environment said that he placed government above big business, individual liberty above government and environment above all.[8] This approach has led the Supreme Court to derive, adopt and apply a range of principles to guide the development of environmental jurisprudence. In *Subhas Kumar vs State of Bihar*[9] the Supreme Court held that the right to life includes the right to enjoy unpolluted atmosphere and if anything endangers or impairs the quality of life in derogation of law, a citizen has a right to move the Supreme Court under Article 32 of the Constitution of India. This theme was reiterated in a town planning case.[10]

There are news of lots of illegal construction by the promoters and developers throughout the country. They are mostly flouting laws and safety norms. "Though the civic body is aware of the developments of such illegal construction, it is yet to initiate any action against the violators."[11] Generally, town planning laws vest discretionary powers in matter of demolition of an illegal building in high officials. The Calcutta High Court has held that such discretion ought to be exercised bonafide and not on extraneous considerations and a circular was issued by the Calcutta Municipal Corporation preventing efforts of regularizing illegal constructions on payment of a fee as penal charges where the structure is otherwise fit for demolition.[12] In *Pratibha Cooperative Housing Society Ltd vs State of Maharastra*[13] the Supreme Court evolved the fundamental norms that stringent action ought to have taken against contumacious defaulters and persons who carry on industrial and developmental activities for profit without regard to environmental laws. A full bench of Punjab and Haryana High Court in *Bakshish Kaur Saini vs Union of India,*[14] by overruling an earlier decision of the court has lain down that unauthorized constructions do not attain legal status by the passage of time. Scope of Judicial Review in environmental cases was explained by the Supreme Court in Calcutta Taj Hotel Case[15] wherein the court referred a balancing approach to be borne in judicial mind whenever dealing with problem of ecology interpreting both the Articles 48A and 51 A (g) of the Constitution of India, considering together and the Supreme Court took a lenient view, in the public benefit in this case as well as in *Rajatha Enterprises vs S.K. Sharma.*[16]

The year 1996 was a landmark in the course of Environmental Jurisprudence. The Public Trust Doctrine was articulated for the first time in India in the case of *M.C. Mehta vs Kamal Nath*[17]. The doctrine has vast potential to serve as a touch stone to test the executive action with a significant environmental impact. The said doctrine is of Roman origin and developed in United States[18] over several years and the Indian Supreme Court has simply imported it and declared that it was a part of the law of the land. The doctrine was founded on the concept that certain common properties like river, forest, sea shore, air etc. were held by the sovereign in trusteeship for free and unimpeded use of the general public and therefore, these natural resources cannot be converted into private ownership. The Supreme Court had the real opportunity to apply this doctrinal principle in *M. I. Builders vs Radhey Shyam Sahu*[19]. Courts analysis of the problems relating to the environment during the year 2002 was more specific than the previous years. The constitutional perspectives were made clearer and provision of certain legislations were scrutinized and explained considering the concept of sustainable development and public trust doctrine and the Court delivered a number of notable judgments. The term sustainable development was subjected to recurrent judicial interpretation in several occasions. The Brundtland Report defined this phrase in terms of development that meets the needs of the present without compromising the ability of the future generation to meet their own needs. In *Vellore Citizens Forum vs U.O.I.*[20] the Supreme Court stated that it is a balancing concept between ecology and development and is seen as a viable concept to eradicate poverty and improve the quality of human life, while living within the carrying capacity of the supporting system. According to Johannesburg Declaration and Programme of Action 2002 economic development, social development, and environmental protection are the three interdependent and mutually reinforcing pillars of sustainable development. Good governance within each country and at the international level is essential for sustainable development. In *Narmada Bachhao Andolan vs U.O.I and others*[21] the apex Court observed that sustainable development means the type of extent of development that can take place and which can be sustained by nature, ecology with or without mitigation .Therefore, the Apex Court's approach to sustainable development was that both the development and environment must go hand in hand and there should not be development at the cost of environment and vice versa.

In 21st Century, the apex Court has not only transformed the principle of 'inter generational equity' and 'sustainable development' into legally enforceable norms but has also defined and explained these norms in the Indian Context and applied them in the facts and circumstances of the cases dealing with all important aspects of environmental law viz. air and water pollution, ecology, wildlife, the heritage and town planning etc., whenever brought before the Court. In *Andhra Pradesh Pollution Control Board vs M.V. Nayndu*[22] the Supreme Court referred to the precautionary principle laid down in Rio Declaration[23] when the Court was really concerned with the question how to avert a serious and irreversible tragedy brought about by development projects not based on environmental expertise.

In recent trends of phenomenal growth of urbanization particularly in constructional activities in and around the cities violation of Floor Space Index (FSI) by the promoters and builders results in direct conflict between ecology and planning. In *Live Oak Resort (P) Ltd. Vs Panchgani Hill Station Municipal Council*[24] the Supreme Court disagreed with the view of the concerned High Court and held that High Court was in error because it has not distinguished the power of the municipal council to sanction or reject the building plan from that of the director of town planning to sanction additional floor space index of the building. The Court viewed that the power of the director as per the byelaws to grant special relaxation supersedes the power of the council and impose a statutory duty on the council to abide by his directions. But the Court added further that the power of the director of town planning in this regard should not lead to adverse impact upon the health of the inhabitants of the locality nor should it violate the fire safety, structural safety and public safety of the building nearby. While delivering such judgment the Supreme Court referred *the People United for Better Living in Calcutta vs State of West Bengal* and *Goa Foundation vs Diksha Holiday(P) Ltd.*

Land is a limited resource and in the present craze of urbanization human settlements are the issues of great concern. The promoters and builders are now encroaching even marshy lands. Water bodies like ponds are now reclaimed by them to convert that into building site in gross violation and disregard to the laws and byelaws. Therefore vanishing water bodies is of great concern and threat to the natural ecosystem. Wetland and water bodies are necessary not only to satisfy the agricultural needs of the locality but also these are very useful to preserve and maintain microclimate of the surrounding. Tanks recharge aquifer in a natural process and therefore, preservation of tanks is very much essential. Can those facilities then be ignored when tanks are filled up and transformed into residential site? This question came up before the Court in *Hench Lal Tiwari vs Kamala Devi*[25] wherein the Supreme Court noticed that spaces which originally were ponds by efflux of time became more or less level lands. The Supreme Court opined that the government and other authorities should have noticed that a pond was falling in disuse and should have bestowed their attention to develop the same. The same question was carefully dealt in while delivering judgment in *Intellectual Forum, Thirupathi vs State of Andhra Pradesh*[26] where the Supreme Court green signaled the decision of conversion, as was taken in public interest to reduce the congestion of Thirupathi Town and as there was no illegality or malafide or arbitrariness. In *People United for Better Living in Calcutta vs State of West Bengal*[27] the Calcutta High Court passed a rational verdict prohibiting the reclamation and use of impugned wetlands for commercial purpose. The Court observed that maintenance of wetlands is necessary as those have a significant role to play in the proper development of society, be it from environmental perspective or from economic perspective. The judgment denotes environmental consciousness and a precautionary approach.

Heritage Conservation is another challenge of modern trends of urbanization. India's heritage treasures bear the testimony of her shared knowledge, expectations, belief, inner conscience and soul of motherland which is our duty as well as the duty of the state to preserve and maintain as enjoined by Articles 49 and 51 A (g) of the Constitution of India. The Supreme Court has rightly observed that right to life extends also to preserving the traditions and cultural heritage of the country and nation.[28]

A green bonanza came the way of Delhi citizens in 1998 when the Supreme Court in *M.C. Mehta vs Union of India*[29] devised a land use pattern balancing the community need against the need of the factory owners who required resources to finance the shifting of industry away from the city to enable the owner of a factory to develop a part of the land for his own benefit and to surrender the reminder for a green belt. Several States have firmed up plans to unlock industrial land to sell for redevelopment.

The Mumbai High Court stunned real estate developers by putting out of their reach 400 acres in the heart of the cramped metropolis. The Court ruled that whenever textile mill land, spanning 600 acres in the city, is sold, one third of it should be kept aside for open spaces and another third for public housing. The two judge's bench also declared invalid the recent sale of five sick national textile corporation owned mills. The verdict came on a public interest litigation filed by the Bombay Environment Action Group which had challenged an order issued by the Vilasrao Deshmukh Government in 2001 that changed Rule 58 of the Development Control Regulations (DCR 58). The said rule 58 which came into force in 1991 laid down the principle of three way division of city mill land during sale and redevelopment. The original rule states that 'the Mill Owners', 'the Brihanmumbai Municipal Corporation' and 'the Maharastra Housing and Development Authority' should get a one-third share wherein the Mill Owners could use their share for commercial development, the Corporation ,for building open spaces and the Development Authority, for public housing or rehabilitating those people who have been displaced by government projects. The order of the Vilasrao Deshmukh Government which amended the said rule in 2001 actually altered a clause to state that only 'open land' excluding the part on which the mill buildings and out builcings stood, was to be divided up in order to derive maximum benefit from the development over the total land. The Bombay High Court remedied the mischief and interpreted that 'open lands' would include lands after demolition of structures and upheld the 1991 provisions.[30] This judgment of the Mumbai High Court has really sent a message to the society and done the job of social engineering to address the causes of poor masses who represent the major part of the democratic resources to enforce their right of housing and casting a duty on the part of the administration to ensure the need of public housing as well as maintaining ecological balances.

The Mumbai high Court's judgment is an epoch making as it has a far reaching consequences in the land and real estate market. The judgment is welcome measure to save the lung of the city. The court has proved its activist role of social engineering by viewing that neglect of the importance of open spaces from the ecological and environmental angle even in congested urban areas can spell doom for the residents of the city and the health of the residents is directly related to the ratio of built up area and open area. The judgment stood against the interest of developers to maximize the profit at the cost of open spaces of the city and the need of the poor masses of their housing and shelter. The verdict has paved the way initiative of community development, an inclusive of social and economic development and reminded the city governments and corporate bodies of their responsibilities and role to preserve urban environments with social and environmental goals.

Now judicial vision is clear that protection is not only the duty of the citizen but it is also the obligation of the state and all other organs including Courts. *Rural Litigation and Enlightenment Kendra, Dehradun vs State of Uttar Pradesh*[31] was the first indication of the right to a wholesome environment which may be traced under Article 21 of the Constitution of India. It has been consistently held by the Supreme Court and the High Courts that the right to a safe environment is implicit in Article 21 of the Constitution of India.[32] Hygienic environment is thus an integral part of healthy life." Right to live with human dignity becomes illusory in the absence of humane and healthy environment"-observed by the Supreme Court in *State of M.P. vs Kedia Leather & Liquor Ltd.*[33]. Thus the Court observed that the 'Environment' represents the 'living space', the 'quality of life' and the very health of human beings including the generation to come. Several High Courts have explicitly recognized an environmental dimension to Article 21 of the Constitution of India. The Andhra pradesh High Court held that it is the legitimate duty of Courts as the enforcing organs of constitutional objectives to forbid all actions of the state and the citizen from upsetting the environmental balance. The High Courts of Rajasthan, Kerala, Himachal Pradesh, Karnataka and Madhya Pradesh too have observed that environmental degradation violates the fundamental right to life.[34] In *Kinkri Devi vs State of Himachal Pradesh*[35] the Court has been guided by the language of Article 48 A of the Constitution of India and observed that Article 14 of Constitution of India may be invoked to challenge government sanctions for activities with high environmental impact where the permissions are arbitrarily granted without adequate consideration of environmental impact. Scope of Judicial Review in environmental cases was explained by the Supreme Court in the Calcutta Taj Hotel case[36] wherein it was observed that whenever a problem of ecology is brought before the court, the Court is bound to bear in mind Article 48 A and Article 51 A (g) of the Constitution of India. The Patna High Court, in *Basudev Yadav vs State of Bihar,* struck[37] a balance and held that for protection of environment, the fundamental right to trade and business under Article 19(1)(g) of the Constitution of India must be read together with the provisions in Article 14,21,48A and 51A(g).

In *M.C. Mehta vs Union of India*[38] the Supreme Court laid emphasis on the provisions in the Constitution to highlight the duty of the state and said that Article 39(c), 47 and 48A collectively cast a duty on the state to secure public health and to protect and improve the environment. During this year i.e. in the year 2002 the Courts invoked and interpreted more provisions in the constitution to protect the environment. The Court relied on Article 162 of the constitution to validate regulations, freed the right to environment from the restriction of property rights under Article 300(A) and made an attempt to expand the frontiers of the writ of mandamus to stop environmental degradation. The Judiciary seems to be ready to issue mandamus even against private persons having a public duty under the nuisance law.

The right to information as an individual and group human right has been recognized in a number of international instruments[39] and is highly relevant to the environment. This right is an essential attribute of the 'democratic process' and 'the principles of popular participation' and therefore, is the key to success of the environment management program and for implementing the laws on the environment. The Supreme Court in *Reliance Petro Chemical Ltd. vs Proprietors of Indian Express Newspapers*[40] has viewed that there is a close link between Article 21 and the 'right to know' particularly where secret government decisions may affect 'health', 'life', and 'livelihood'. Reiterating this principle in *Essar Oil Ltd.*[41] case, the Supreme Court also emphasized the role of voluntary organizations in the environment management. The Court has interpreted that Article 51 A(g) of the Constitution of India makes the citizen responsible for protection of the environment and it is, therefore, necessary that citizen has a 'right to know'.

Thus post 1990's development in the field of environmental management shows a metamorphosis in perception of Development from its economic necessity driven by market force to its desired socio-environmental goal as have been studied by different branches. The Indian Judiciary has also been influenced by the concept of alternative approach of development. Displaying a certain degree of judicial activism the Supreme Court has recognized that though 'right to development' and 'right to life'- both spring from the same constitutional premises i.e., Article 21 of the Constitution, the development only driven by the economic necessity cannot override the right to life of the citizens which is placed above. The social and economic development should be encouraged. The Judiciary has voiced for active citizenship which prioritizes collective responsibilities and common goals; how much we should prepared to sacrifice for our future generations. In urban environments with their large ecological footprints such questions are imperative and demanding. They require civic and ecological literacy or an understanding of governmental and environmental processes. This is why effective participation in decision making process and for that capacity building is essential in order to get collective outcome for a better quality of life. The Supreme Court has, therefore, emphasized on the environmental awareness and duty to spread environmental education as was observed in *Andhra Pradesh Pollution Control Board vs M.V. Naydu*. The Indian Judiciary thus has developed a rich corpus of cultural heritage and environmental jurisprudence by applying the principles of sustainable development, intergenerational equity, the precautionary principle and public trust doctrine approach in determining and applying the environmental laws in various developmental issues wherever ecological threat and right to life of the citizens are involved. Lastly, it is to be concluded that in a wide range of developmental activities including adopting a land use change or the use of agricultural land for non agricultural purposes, wherein citizen's fundamental right under Article 21 of the Constitution of India has been violated and ecological balance is disturbed, the Judiciary has become 'enthusiastic environmentalist' and has adopted a balancing approach reconciling environment and development. Indian Judiciary by adopting, applying and transforming those Doctrines into an integral part of Indian Law has showed the path to perceive 'Development' in an inclusive sense of improvement linking all aspects of human welfare like natural, social, economic, and political in a given society.

Notes

1. Article 48A of the Constitution of India.
2. Article 32 of the Constitution of India.
3. AIR 1986 Gujarat 50.
4. AIR 1974 SC 2177.
5. Divan, Shyam and Armin Roscencranz. Environmental Law and Policy in India, p. 323.
6. AIR 1987 A.P. 171, 181.
7. Divan, Shyam and Armin Roscencranz. Environmental Law and Policy in India, p. 393.
8. *Ibid.*, p. 41.
9. AIR 1991 SC 420, 424
10. Virendra Gaur vs State of Haryana 1995(2) SCC 577
11. Published in The Telegraph Calcutta, Tuesday 6th February 2007(METRO)
12. Land & Bricks & Entertainment Ltd. Vs State of W.B. 1991(2) Cal. H. N. 306
13. AIR 1991 SC 1453, 1456.
14. AIR 1994 P & H 1.
15. Sachidananda Pandey vs State of West Bengal, AIR 1987 SC 1109, 1115.
16. AIR 1989 SC 860.

17. AIR 1997(1) SCC 388.
18. National Audubon Society vs Superior Court of Alpine Country [33 cal 3d 419], popularly known as Mono Lake Case wherein the Supreme Court of California applied the doctrine to show the judicial concern In protecting all ecologically important lands
19. AIR 1999 SC 2468.
20. AIR 1996 sc 2715 at 2720.
21. (2000) 10 SCC 664.
22. AIR 1999 SC 812.
23. Principle 15 of the Rio Declaration.
24. (2000) 8 SCC 329 at 331, 332.
25. (2001) 6 SCC 496.
26. AIR 2006 SC 1350.
27. AIR 1993 Cal 215.
28. Consumer Education and Research Centre vs Union of India, AIR 1995 SC 922,959
29. 1996(4) SCC 351
30. The Telegraph, 17th October 2005, Special Correspondent, Mumbai
31. AIR 1998 SC 2187.
32. M.C.Mehta vs Union of India AIR 1991 SC 1132; M.C.Mehta vs Union of India AIR 1998 SC 2693; Consumer Education and Research Centre vs Union of India AIR 1995 SC 922
33. (2003) 7 SCC 398 at 394
34 . (a) L.K. Koolwal vs. State of Rajasthan, AIR 1988 Raj. 2, 4.

  (b) Arvind Textiles vs. State of Rajasthan, AIR 1994 Raj. 195, 197.

  (c) Law Society of India vs. Fertilizers and Chemicals Travancore Ltd. AIR 1994 Ker 308, 370.

  (d) V. Lakshmipathy vs. State of Karnataka AIR 1994 Kar 57, 67

  (e) Hamid Khan vs. State of Madhya Pradesh, AIR 1997 MP 191, 193
34. AIR 1988 H. P. 4, 9.
35. Sachidananda Pandey vs. State of West Bengal, AIR 1987 SC 1109, 1115.
36. AIR 2002 Pat 64
37. AIR 2002 SC 1696
38. Universal Declaration of Human Rights, Article, 19.

The International Covenant on Civil and Political Rights.

Stockholm Declaration, Principle 19.

The Rio Declaration, Principle 10.

The World Charter of Nature 1982.

UNESCO Convention for the Protection of the WORLD Culture and Natural Heritage,1972.

39. AIR 1989 SC 190, 202.

40. Essar Oil Ltd. vs. Haldar Utakarsh Samiti, AIR 2004 SC 1834.

Right to Medical Assistance and Constitution of India

GANESH JI TIWARI* & SANJAY KUMAR SINGH**

INTRODUCTION

RIGHT to health is guaranteed under Article 21 of the constitution of India. This right has been couched in the negative term and when read literally it empowers the State to interfere with the enjoyment of life and liberty according to produce established by law.

The jurisprudence of personhood or philosophy of the right to life envisaged under Article 21 enlarges its sweep to encompass human personality in its full bloom with invigorated health which is a wealth to the workmen to earn his livelihood to sustain the dignity of person and to live a life with dignity and equality.

Right to health and medical care to protect health and vigour, while in service or after retirement was held a fundamental right of a worker under Article 21, read with Articles 38(1), 39(e), 41, 42, 43, 47 and all related constitutional provisions and fundamental human rights to make the life of the workman meaningful and purposeful with dignity of person. The right to health of a worker is an integral facet of meaningful right to life, to have not only a meaningful existence but also robust health and vigour without which the worker would economic necessity to work in an industry exposed to health hazards, due to indigence for bread-winning for

* Lecturer Selection Grade, Sikkim Govt. Law College, Burtuk, Gangtok Sikkim.

** Faculty, Department of Law, University of North Bengal District Darjeeling- 734013 and Research Scholar, Department of Law, Burdwan University, W.B.

himself and his dependent, should not be at the; cost of the health and vigour of the workman.

RIGHT TO LIFE AND PERSONAL LIBERTY INCLUDES RIGHT TO HEALTH AND MEDICAL ASSISTANCE

In *Paramanand Katara v. Union of India*[1], the Supreme Court shaped right to health as fundamental right under Article 21 of the Constitution. The instant case was filed under Article 32 as a PIL when a private doctor refused to treat a patient who met with an accident because of non-compliance of procedural formalities regarding accident victims. The court ordered the medical institutions to provide medical aid and treatment immediately irrespective of whether the procedural formalities have been complied with. The patient whether he can be an innocent person or a criminal liable to punishment under the laws of the society, it is the obligation of those who are in charge of the health of the community to preserve life so that the innocent maybe protected and the guilty may be punished. Article 21 of the Constitution casts the obligation on the state to preserve life.

The Court directed that in order to make everyone aware of this position the decision of the Court must be published in all journals reporting decisions of this Court and adequate publicity highlighting these aspects should be given by the national media. The Medical Council must be send copies of the Judgment to every medical college affiliated to it. This is a very significant ruling of the Court. Law has to help and not to take way life within its boundaries. Any talk of human rights or right to life would be an empty slogan if right to health is subordinate or ignored by the legal system. Therefore, *Paramanand Katara* assumes more dynamic and live significant in shaping right to health as a fundamental right.

In recent past the Supreme Court had an opportunity to enquire into the lethargic attitude of the Government in providing sophisticated medical facilities in *Paschim Banga Khet Mazdoor Samiti v. State of West Bengal*[2] by following Paramanand Katara's ruling the Supreme Court has held that denial of medical aid by government's hospitals to an injured person on the ground of non-availability of beds amounted to violation of right to life under Article 21 of the Constitution. In this case, the petitioner Hakim

Sheikh, who was a member of an organization of agricultural laborers', had fallen from a running train and had suffered serious head injuries and brain hemorrhage. He was taken to various government hospitals in the city of Calcutta but because of non-availability of bed he was not admitted. Ultimately he was admitted in a private hospital as an indoor patient and he had to incur an expenditure of Rs. 17,000 in his treatment. The Supreme Court held that Article 21 imposes an obligation on the state to provide medical assistance to every injured person. Preservation of human life is of paramount importance. Failure on the part of the government hospital to provide timely medical treatment to a person in need of such treatment results in violation of his right to life guaranteed under Article 21 of the constitution. The Court directs the state to pay Rs. 25,000 to the petitioner as compensation.

In the historic judgment in *Consumer Education & Research Centre V. Union of India*[3] the Supreme Court held that the right to health and medical care is a fundamental right under Article 21 of the Constitution as it is essential for making the life of the workmen meaningful and purposeful with dignity of person. "Right to life" in Article 21 includes protection of the health and strength to the worker. The expression life under Article 21 does not connote mere animals' existence. It has a much wider meaning which includes right to livelihood, better standard of life, hygienic conditions in workplace and leisure.

In *Kirloskar Brothers Ltd. V. Employees'State Insurance Corpn*[4], the Supreme Court, following the judgment of Consumer Education & Research Centre's case, has held that 'right to health' is a fundamental right of the workmen. The Court also health that this right is not only available against the state and its instrumentalities but even private industries to ensure to the workmen to provide facilities and opportunities for health and vigour of workman assured in the provision of Part IV of the constitution which are integral part of right to equality under Art. 14 and right to invigorated life under Art.21 which are fundamental rights to the workmen.

In *State of Punjab v. Mohinder Singh Chawal*[5] the respondent, an employee of the State government of Punjab, had a heart aliment. Since the facility of the treatment was not available in the state hospital of Punjab, he was given permission by the director with the approval of the medical board, to get the treatment outside the state. The respondent had the treatment in the AIIMS, at New Delhi. While granting reimbursement for the actual expenses incurred, the appellant rejected his bill for room rent paid to the paid to the paid to the hospital as inadmissible. The question before the Supreme Court were whether while reimbursing the medical expenses the room rent paid to the hospital was to be included or not. Allowing the contention of the employee, the Supreme Court held that if the government servant had suffered an aliment which required treatment at a specialized approved hospital, it was the duty of the state to bear the expenditure incurred by the government servant. Thus the employee was entitled to the room rent actually paid by him to the hospital.

RIGHT TO PRIVACY

In *State of Maharastra v. Madhulkar Narain*[6], it has been held that the 'right to privacy' is available even to a woman of easy virtue and no one can invade her privacy. A police Inspector visited the house of one *Banubai* in uniform and demanded to have sexual intercourse with her. On refusing he tried to have her by force. She raised a hue and cry. When he was prosecuted he told the Court that she was a lady of easy virtue and therefore her evidence was not to be relied. The Court rejected the argument of the applicant and held him liable for violating her right to privacy under Article 21 of the Constitution.

In *Suriit Singh Thind v. Kanwaliit Kaur,*[7] it was held that Medical examination of a woman for her virginity amounts to violation of her right to privacy and personal liberty enshrined under Article 21 of the Constitution. In this case the wife has filed a petition for decree of nullity of marriage on the ground that the marriage has never been consummated because the husband was impotent. The husband has taken the defense that the marriage was consummated and he had not impotent. In order to prove that the wife was not virgin the husband filed an application for her medical examination. The Court held that the allowing the medical examination of a woman's virginity violates her right to privacy under Article 21 of the Constitution. Such an order would amounts to roving enquiry against a female who is vulnerable even otherwise. The virginity test cannot constitute the sole basis, to prove the consummation of marriage.

In *Ms X v. Mr. Z*[8], the wife filed a petition for dissolution of marriage on the ground of cruelty and adultery against husband under Section 10 of Divorce Act. The husband also asserted that his wife had adulterous affairs with one person which resulted in family way the pregnancy of wife was terminated at All India Institute of Medical Sciences and records and slides of tabular gestation were preserved in the hospital. The husband filed an application for seeking DNA test of the said slides with a view to ascertain if the husband is the father of the foetus. The court held that the right to privacy, though a fundamental right, forming part of right to life enshrined under Act 21 is not an absolute right. When the right to privacy has become a part of public document, in that case the person cannot insist that such DNA test would infringe his or her right to privacy. The foetus was no longer a part of body and when it has been preserved in AIIMS the wife who had already discharged the same cannot claim that it affects her right of privacy. When adultery has been alleged to be one of the grounds of divorce in such circumstances the application of the husband seeking DNA test of the said slides can be allowed.

RIGHT TO MEDICAL ASSISTANCE UNDER THE DIRECTIVE PRINCIPLES OF STATE POLICY

Social order based on justice: Article 38(1) of the Constitution of India provide that the state shall strive to promote the welfare of the people by securing and protecting as effectively as it may, a social order in which justice - social, economic and political- shall inform all the institution of national life.

Principles of policy to be followed by the state for securing economic justice: Article 39 (e) provides that to protect health and strength of worker and tender age of children and to ensure that they are not forced by economics necessity to enter avocations unsuited to their age or strength.

Right to work, education and public assistance in certain cases: Article 41 directs the state to ensure the people within the limit of its economic capacity and development: (a) employment (b) education and (c) public assistance in cases I of unemployment, old age, sickness and disablement and in other cases of undeserved want.

Just and human conditions of work: Article 42 directs the state to make provision for securing just human conditions and maternity relief.

Duty to raise the standard of living and improvement of health: Article 47 imposes duty upon the State to raise the level of nutrition and the standard of living of its people and the improvement of public health. In particular, the State should bring about prohibition of the consumption except for medical purposes of intoxications drinks and drugs which are injurious to health.

CONCLUSION

After analyzing all the various aspects and judicial cases I can come to the conclusion that medical assistance has become a part of Article 21 of the Constitution. The approach in Paschim Banga is more remarkable because the State of the Central Governments is directed to provide basic medical treatment. In the present scenario, since, the life of the person can be effectively preserved from physical retardation with the aid of medical technology developments, along with the private institution the government has to come forward to equip the State run medical institution with sophisticated medical instruments to render medical assistance. The Government may face financial constraint in implementing all these laudable directions but that should not be an excuse for the state to provide cheap medicine and drugs, better equipped hospitals with modernized medical technological facilities and these things have to be done by the state in accordance with the international declaration, mandate of the constitution and the judicial observation.

It is true that plethora of complaints of corporate and super specialty Hospital fleecing the patient and too much of commercialization at the expense of hapless patients are pouring in. The improvement of public health being one of the Directive Principles and the evolution of proper Medicare system under which the people can have the medical treatment free from exploitation will be in furtherance of the fundamental right to life enshrined in Article 21 of the Constitution, there is paramount need for the State to focus its attention to these aspects and find remedial measures. Although the Consumer Protection Act provides sufficient safeguard and remedial against exploitation of patients, that is only one facet of grievance redressal, but that is not the be all and end all. The existing laws are either inadequate or deficient. It is time that the State should take stock of the situation, if not ready done and initiate necessary measures such as setting up a grievance redressal machinery and devising a regulatory mechanism to cover vulnerable areas where unfair and unprofessional practices are rampant. If necessary, the State should not hesitate to enact comprehensive practices are rampant.

Notes

1. AIR 1989 SC 2039.
2. (1996) 4 SCC 37.
3. (1995) 3 SCC 42.
4. (1996) 2 SCC 682.
5. AIR 1997 SC 1225.
6. AIR1991SC 207.
7. AIR 2003 P&H 353.
8. AIR 2002 Del. 217.

Socio-Economic Rights are Human Rights: Unfolding the Myth

UDAY SHANKAR*

INTRODUCTION

HUMAN rights are quest of every civilization. Human rights are rights of individual to live with dignity regardless of social, economic and political status.[1] Human rights inherently constitute of elements relating to freedom and conditions necessary to enjoy that freedom. Rights are designed in a hierarchy on account of the obligations of the state and nature of rights. Rights requiring non-interventionists state are termed as civil and political rights whereas rights warranting resources for realization are termed as social and political rights. Former relates to autonomy of an individual, later relates to conditions of enjoyment of autonomy.

Social and economic rights are rights relating to sustenance and means of livelihood which depends, arguably, upon the availability of resources and formulation of policies. Social and economic rights are essential for guaranteeing well-being and dignified to human being. Social and economic rights are intertwined and interlinked due to nature of rights and process realization involved therein. Social rights are necessarily having economic influence in their contour and economic rights are inherently linked with social aspect of individual and society.

---

* *Assistant Professor of Law at Rajiv Gandhi School of Intellectual Property Law, Indian Institute of Technology Kharagpur, (shankarudaymishra@gmail.com.)*

Undisputedly, these rights are inherent and indispensable for dignified existence of human being. The hierarchical structure amongst rights created split in human rights discourse. This hierarchy, willingly or unwillingly, created a gap between two groups of rights. Human rights discourse started focusing on realization of civil and political rights reducing social and economic rights dependent upon policies and programme of state. The 'resource-related' principle of obligation of state in the matter of enforcement of social and economic rights threatened the place of these rights in the league of human rights. The argument of non-universal, need based and situational requirement affected the status and position of these rights.[2]

The differential treatment in realization of social and economic rights resulted into marginalization of these rights to the extent of existence as a right in the right based discourse. The paper attempts to unfold the myth surrounding socio-economic rights and establishes that they are quintessential for dignified existence of human being. The paper is divided into six parts. The second part examines the universal nature of these rights, third part negates argument of divisibility between the two group of rights on the basis of nature of obligations. The fourth part relates vagueness and socio-economic rights in order to examine tenability of argument of *aspirational* status for these rights. The fifth section deals with importance of resources in examining the enforcement of these rights. The paper concludes with the proposition that socio-economic rights are rights in scheme of human rights and denial of status of rights would amount to distortion and destruction of human rights discourse.

SOCIO-ECONOMIC RIGHTS AND UNIVERSALITY

Social and economic rights are contested as rights on the ground of non-universal nature. Cranston has argued that a right to be properly termed as a right, it must pass the test of "universality", with it being asserted that for this test to be satisfied the right claimed must impose a universal duty, so that it can be claimed as a right against all. A traditional negative right, such as freedom of expression, which demands only non-interference, can intelligibly be asserted against the world at large.[3] Even the civil and political rights are not universal in their applicability. They warrant specific situation for their implementation. For instance, the right to be presumed innocent until proven guilty[4] is held only by those charged with a penal offence. The political rights are, generally, conferred upon citizens of the nation. The acquisition of citizenship is qualified with fulfillment of certain conditions in every country. Additionally, this argument can be countered by an example, it can be said that all children have the right to be cared for, so that right is universal to all children even though, for a particular child, the corresponding duty falls upon their parents/guardians. By analogy, socio-economic rights may be asserted on behalf of all humans but the duty to provide those goods fall upon their particular society.[5]

Another argument against the universality of socio-economic rights is scarcity of resources. It is simply not the case that the needs of all can be met and, therefore, is not true that all the needy have rights to the resources necessary to meet those needs. This conflict of rights inter se individuals is not peculiar with the socio-economic rights. Right to freedom of speech and expression may result into conflict with the rights of others.[6] The realization one component of civil and political rights might lead to renouncement of exercise of the other component. Hence the discourse of rights may result into conflict and certain elements of conflict must be regarded as more or less inevitable.[7] The conflict is more in socio-economic rights due to their nature. But such conflict is not sufficient to take away the universal character of these rights.

SOCIO-ECONOMIC RIGHTS AND NEGATIVE RIGHTS

Socio-economic rights are distinguished from civil and political rights in more than one way. One of the major arguments for such distinction is the normative character of socio-economic rights. Socio-economic rights are considered as positive rights whereas civil and political rights are negative rights. The distinction between negative and positive rights mirrors the traditional division between civil and political rights, which restrain the state from intruding; and socio-economic rights, which elicit the protection by the State against want or need.[8] The categorization of rights can be related to nature of governmental action. Negative liberty requires non-intervention whereas positive liberty requires significant contribution from state. The obligation of state to provide resources has been accepted as distinguishing factor. It is claimed that civil and political rights do not invite any positive action from state. These in turn reflect two distinct views of liberty: liberty as freedom from state interference; liberty as freedom from want and fear.[9]

The precise nature of civil and political rights assists courts to enforce the rights effectively. 'Negative' rights are accepted as cost-free rights. The duties entailed in 'negative rights' are specific and can be performed simultaneously. State is obliged to perform the duty of not interfering with everyone who has the right not to be interfered with. The duties are not clear like duties of civil and political rights. The nature of rights warrants immediate implementation. Moreover, State will not have any difficulty in committing itself for these rights. State is only required to stay away from the legitimate activities of individuals.

This dichotomy is based on oversimplification of rights. The arguments of positive and negative rights are untenable. The distinction based on this dichotomy is false and founded on misconception. The obligation of state in regard to fulfillment of human rights are overemphasized and stretched too far to create an artificial boundary between the two groups of rights. The obligation of state in implementing rights is the same. It varies only in degree and stages of obligation for various rights. Though, the domestic tribunals have reflected their willingness to enforce these rights through judicial process.[10] Disputing the contention of non-competence of judiciary to enforce these rights, an alternative forum may be suggested to enforce these rights.

The distinction between 'negative' and 'positive' rights draws much of its support from the nature of obligation of state. The philosophical development in this area repudiates the distinction on this basis. The idea of tripartite obligation negates the basis of distinction. The idea of tripartite typology of state obligations with respect to human rights was originally introduced in 1980 by Henry Shue, who spoke of obligations 'to avoid depriving', to protect from deprivation' and 'to aid the deprived'.[11] However, it is Asbje Eide who has become originator of the tripartite terminology, as we know it today, in the slightly different version of obligations to respect, protect and fulfill, which he originally introduced in 1987 when he functioned as the Special Rapporteur to the UN

Sub-Commission.[12] The idea of this obligation was initiated to do away with the misleading distinction based on 'negative and 'positive' character of rights and nature of obligations. Eide argued that we cannot 'make a neat distinction around the axis of "negative/positive" between civil and political rights on the one hand and socio-economic rights on the other.'[13] Instead he suggested that State responsibility be examined at three levels, going from the predominantly cost-free and passive obligation to respect, to the gradually more active and costly obligations to protect and to fulfill.

The nature of obligations suggested by Shue and further concretized by Eide weakens the argument of divisibility of rights on 'positive and negative' grounds. State obligations require all human rights to be realized through three various steps suggested. There are social and economic rights which do not require any resource for its implementation. The obligation to *respect* obliges the state to avoid depriving a human being of dignified existence in situations where that status has been attained. The obligations to *protect* oblige the state to prevent third parties from depriving a human being of dignified status in situations where the status has been attained. The obligations to *fulfill* oblige a State to secure the dignified status/existential status for human beings in situation where that has not been attained. The obligation to respect does not demand any deployment of resources, the obligation to protect may demand some (mainly infrastructural) resources and a complicated obligation to fulfill may have to deploy both infrastructural and material sources.[14]

The three categories of obligations require for civil and political rights as well as for socio-economic rights. However, the governments have largely ignored obligations to fulfill in the case of socio-economic rights and obligations to protect in case of civil and political rights. The crime is rising on newer scales due to failure of government to protect civil and political rights from third parties. The categories of obligations reflect the difference in degree of state obligations and not in substance. Human rights differ only in the relative importance of different categories in their spectrum of obligations. And this importance may depend on the specific historical and geographic situation. Hence, the argument of realization of civil and political rights at the first instance may not fulfill the goal of human rights. The fulfillment of rights varies from society to society. Ill-treatment to socio-economic rights on the ground of resources would certainly jeopardize the very growth of idea of human rights on which modern world is trying to sustain.

Socio-economic rights need not always invite resources for its implementation. Certain socio-economic rights can be effectively ensured by mere non-interventionists approach of state. The rights can be implemented without any action from state. It fulfills the requisites of civil and political rights, if I may say so. For instance, right to form trade unions, right to strike, to count a few, do not invite any budgetary allocation from the state for their implementation. It is pertinent to note that the General Comment of Committee on Economic, Social and Cultural Rights, in General Comment No. 3 observed that the there are socio-economic rights which "would seem to be capable of immediate application by judicial and other organs in many legal systems." These rights, it says, include equal rights of men and women, equal pay for equal work, the right to form trade unions and the right to strike, the right of children to special protection, the right to primary education, the right to choose a non-public school, the liberty to establish schools, and the freedom for scientific research and creative activity.[15] In General Comment No. 4 the Committee has included the right to housing as well.[16] On the other hand, certain civil and political rights require state to spend money for its effective realization. State needs to establish infrastructure for wholesome enjoyment of some civil and political rights. In the absence of allocation of resources, such rights will be meaningless. They resemble the characteristics of socio-economic rights, if I may say so. For instance, right to fair trial, right to legal aid, to name a few, warrant State to establish institutions like court, prisons, prosecution, for its effective implementation.

Therefore, the tripartite terminology bridges the two set of rights by illustrating that compliance with each and every human rights may require various measures from (passive) non interference to (active) ensuring of the satisfaction of individual needs, all depending on concrete circumstances. Different stages of obligations play a role in effective implementation of rights in general. It would be false to categories rights on such grounds. It is pertinent to mention here the observation of the South African Constitutional Court regarding negative obligation of state for realizing socio-economic rights. In a 1996 decision regarding certification of the legality of its new constitution, the South African Constitutional Court reasoned that the constitutional guarantees of socio-economic rights "... at the very minimum... can be negatively protected from improper invasion".[17]

Civil and political rights give rise to only negative duties are partially correct. They may give rise to negative duties, positive duties, or both. On the one hand they prevent state action securing a zone of personal freedom in which one is allowed to do what one wants. On the other hand, they may require state action securing the opportunities and resources necessary to the achievement of freedom, a condition in which one is able to do what one wants. Or they may do both these things, preventing state action and requiring others.[18] For instance, the traditional right to freedom of expression can be exercised by preventing state to not to interfere in the exercise of it. The freedom may see threat in a situation of opposition of expression by fundamentalist within the society. In such a case, state is required to extend all available means to the individual in exercise of the freedom. Only non-intervention of state would not lead to enjoyment of guaranteeing freedom. Just as it is possible to understand civil and political rights in positive terms, so it is possible to understand economic rights in negative terms.

The tripartite obligations deprive the argument of distinguishing two set of rights on the normative character of positive and negative rights. To further weaken the distinction based on negative and positive rights, other legal scholars evolved the idea of four kinds of obligations. Thus van Hoof speaks of obligations to respect, to protect, to ensure and to promote.[19] Taking the matter further, Steiner and Alston are supportive of a quintuple set of obligations. They speak of obligations: (1) to respect rights of others; (2) to create institutional machinery essential to realization of rights; (3) to protect rights/ prevent violations; (4) to provide goods and services to satisfy rights; and (5) to promote rights.[20] A common feature is, however, that all suggestions as to the most suitable typology move along a continuum from 'negative' to more 'positive' obligations, inserting an obligation to protect from interferences from third parties in between.[21]

The denial of status of rights on the basis of obligation of state in implementation of rights is negated. The obligation of the state is the same for all human rights. It is only the degree of obligation that varies as per the nature of rights. It would be unjust to deny status of human rights to social and economic rights on the ground of degree of obligation. The different degree of obligation only establishes different natures of rights. It cannot be stretched to the extent of denial of existence as rights. State is obliged to enforce all human rights irrespective of its nature. The general duty to realize these rights are on state governments. The duties are also on international organizations to support the effort of individual governments in realization of these rights. Interestingly, the Indian Constitution adds a new dimension in fulfillment of these rights by entrusting duties on citizens.[22] The utility of fundamental duties in making social and economic rights a reality for masses is an unexplored area.

SOCIO-ECONOMIC RIGHTS AND VAGUENESS

Human rights are values of human ends. Core of human ends are indeterminate. Human values differ from society to society and individual to individual. It is difficult to universalize all values. Some values are universalized as rights. Hence, all the cores could not find their place in the protected and respected language of rights. The pluralistic pattern structures the language of rights in different categories depending on its values. Every core of human value cannot be legalized and confer protection due to inherent conflict and vagueness into it. Some of the core values are given privileged status in the form of rights over other values. These privileged values are assigned through rights. The legal document categorizes certain core values based on the pattern of society and values of the society. Normative characters are given to these cores to avoid conflict between competing values. They reduce the scope of attaching meaning to these values in adjudication process by the courts. Therefore, they remain valid in democratic structure where the contents are not defined by the unaccountable judiciary.

The normative character are attributed to values, priorities are conferred upon them. In study of human rights, civil and political rights are given precedence over social and economic rights. The precedence to particular rights over other rights is highly contestable in the absence of universally accepted formula to determine it.[23] Vagueness and non-specificity is common phenomenon of all rights which comprises of human values. The concept of human rights are said to be an essentially contestable.

The legal scholars allegedly, refused, to grant due status to socio-economic right on the basis of vagueness and abstract nature. The doctrine of indivisibility of different categories of rights is affected by non-specific and want of precise content of socio-economic rights. The argument of vagueness was further strengthened on ground of nature of obligations of State. It is very difficult to give contents to these groups of rights due to varying socio-economic needs of individuals. These rights are open-ended in contrast with negative rights which are clear and specific. Negative rights require state to abstain from certain activities. The obligations of state are very specific and also violability can be examined in uniform and universal way. It is contended that civil and political rights require exact degree of protection whereas socio-economic rights is a matter of politics and policy. Civil and political rights differentiate clearly between forbearance and omission and consequently the duties which flow from such rights are unambiguous.

Rights entail duties but people can only logically have a duty to do something in so far as this is possible to perform. However, given the insatiable nature of social rights and the prevailing conditions in developing countries, it is not possible for the governments to provide all members of such a society with rights to socio-economic goods. It is therefore an empty claim to assert that all those inhabitants have such rights, these results in the fact that such rights are socially relative.[24] These rights are accepted as duties on state to promote material needs of individual without conferring claim-right upon individuals. Hence, it is seen as "programmatic and promotional" in nature.

The vague natures of socio-economic rights are taken as one of the reasons for non-enforceability of these rights. Courts have refused to entertain alleged violations of these rights, reasoning that its "boundless and indeterminate principles" resist judicial conception.[25] Their vagueness functions as a negative feedback cycle, both resulting from and causing the perception of non-justiciability: These rights are vague because they are non-justiciable, and this non-justiciability prevents judges from applying them and developing a jurisprudence that clarifies their content.[26] The vagueness is closely linked with the perception of the obligations of protect and fulfill which is to be determined on societal development. It is always related to positive obligations of state. Courts have more difficulty monitoring a government's obligation to take positive steps than its duty simply not to interfere with individual's existing entitlements.[27] Socio-economic rights are termed as positive rights which require an action from state for its realization. Most positive rights are different in that their enforcement calls for government actions which are not fully determined by those rights, which are subject to policy choices, amenable to criteria of expediency and exposed to public debate. Hence the courts are not competent actors for their enforcement.[28]

The suggested schemes of implementation of socio-economic rights also add to the argument of vagueness. The "progressive realization" contributes to the vagueness of socio-economic rights since states can never be sure of exactly what their obligations are at any particular time.[29] The implementation of these rights has been associated with economic progress of a nation. Therefore, their implementations are left on the will of policy makers. The duty-holder expresses reluctance in enforcing these rights on the pretext of imprecise nature of obligations.

The idea that social and economic rights are inherently as indeterminate as to be incapable of judicial enforcement by the courts is belied by the increasing body of jurisprudence relating to such rights at the international, regional and national levels. It has been rebutted in scholarship and in practice; the socio-economic rights are incapable of determinate content and specific obligations. Specifically, the CESCR has issued a series of General Comments that support the capacity of many socio-economic rights for interpretation,[30] and it has adopted a twin track approach of identifying a "minimum core" standard (required for all states), and requiring "maximization" (whereby a state must take all reasonable steps to realise the standard set of rights).

The reasons of indeterminate nature of socio-economic rights contributed to step-brotherly treatment towards them. The judicial creativity seen in the affair of civil and political rights is distinctly missing in the case of socio-economic rights. As Sandra Liebenberg has pointed out, "It is through recourse to the conventions of constitutional interpretation and their application to the facts of different cases that the specific content and scope of a right emerges with greater clarity ... The fact that the content of many social and economic rights is less well-defined than civil and political rights is more a reflection of their exclusion from processes of adjudication than of their inherent nature."[31] Alston rightly rejects the argument of attaching vagueness only with socio-economic rights by stating that

> "Going back to 1948 and the adoption of the Universal Declaration, questions such as 'what is meant by fair trial?' and How do we define what constitutes inhuman, degrading treatment or punishment?' would have revealed civil and political rights to be every bit as open-ended, vague and indeterminate as the meaning of a right to health today. One of the differences is that human rights organisations, groups and individuals have been worrying away at definitions and applications of civil and political rights for the past fifty years."[32]

Indeed, there are strong arguments in favour of open-textured framing of all human rights, so that courts are able to respond adequately to individual circumstances and historical developments in concretising their meaning over time.

Moreover, the argument of non-justiciability has been negative by the introduction of three kinds of obligations for all the rights. The obligations to respect, protect, and fulfil the claim of an individual rejects 'programmatic' allegation of socio-economic rights. It is untenable that socio-economic rights can be realised by pouring in of resources, certain rights may be respected by non-intervention of the state. Of course, there are socio-economic rights which require state to spend resources; it does not take away the character of rights.

Many civil and political rights, such as the right to life, the right to equality are vague and open-textured in their formulation. Some social and economic rights, in comparison, are given relatively more precision. For example, the right to the highest attainable standard of health in the ICESCR makes specific reference to infant mortality, "environmental and industrial hygiene",[33] and the "treatment and control of epidemic, endemic, occupational and other diseases"[34] while the right to education specifically refers to the requirement that primary education be compulsory and free.[35] Preciseness and specificity of certain civil and political rights are determined on the basis of other relevant factors. For instance, the content of rights guaranteed under Article 19(1) of the Constitution of India is determined in reference to factors laid down in clause 2 of Article 19.[36] The amount of protection right to freedom of speech will get depends upon the situation of security of state or factors relating to contempt of judicial process.

Open ended human rights will be helpful in deducing other human rights and benefit the human rights discourse in larger perspective. Many rights are evolved in the process of interpretation of rights. Right to equality includes equal pay for equal work,[37] right to life includes right against sexual exploitation of women at work place,[38] right to freedom to carry on trade, profession and commerce includes right to trade on pavement[39].

Civil and political rights and social and economic rights express some ultimate value itself or a fundamental corollary thereof; yet they are both incompatible and incommensurable, and their incommensurability makes it impossible to say how much of each right the best society would contain or would give most value to individual lives. If there is no way of choosing between or balancing between, then, for those reasons, there cannot be a rational basis for prioritizing one set of rights, for example the negative liberties of intellectual and economic freedom as the legal guarantees favoring scientific advancement, artistic creativity and/or economic efficiency and progress, over alternative economic rights favoring the goal of equality or the satisfaction of basic needs. Choosing the former favors one value and choosing the latter favors the other, but since there is no rational way of establishing the priority of either underlying value, there is no rational basis for prioritizing one set of rights over another. Contrary to much wishful thinking, rights cannot be neutral, and there can be no higher-order rational or moral criteria in trade-offs between rights which express or are essential to the safeguarding or realization of rivalrous human ends.[40]

From the perspective of value pluralism, the privileged defend the status assigned to civil and individual liberties, but denied to the values of social justice or minimum needs, lacks a normative basis and cannot be defended on rational grounds. Unless one is prepared to endorse the premises that individual liberty is a higher value than equality in any form, that negative liberty generally trumps positive liberty and that the primacy of individual liberty over other values goes so far as to ground a general priority of negative liberties over social rights which finds its acknowledged limit only in the need for general protection of the minimum social and psychological conditions of individual agency, the primacy assigned to civil and political rights is morally arbitrary.[41]

Branding complete range of socio-economic rights as imprecise and vague would be injustice. And also denial of vagueness of such rights would amount to non-acceptance of truth. There are precise and specific rights in socio-economic rights as well. It is unfair to attribute vagueness only to socio-economic rights. The rights are vague in terms of specific obligation of state. The problem of vagueness can be addressed by identifying minimum threshold of every right. Accordingly, an obligation can be imposed upon states for their realisation. It can not be a ground to denial of status of right to these rights. They are still rights, but their imperfection is a challenge to legal creativity.

SOCIO-ECONOMIC RIGHTS AND RESOURCES

One of the major factors of distinction between civil and political rights and social and economic rights is based on resources. Need of resources in implementation of rights play crucial role in attaching priority to a group of rights over other group rights. Resources are related with the role of state in fulfillment of these rights. Rights must be read with remedies. The effectiveness of remedy depends upon the resources available with state. Hence, determines the characteristics of rights. It is contended that the requirement of expenditure by state extracts the character of rights from socio-economic rights. Civil and political rights do not require any cost in their implementation. State needs to stay away from the exercise of liberty by an individual. In case of socio-economic rights, it is argued that need based rights cannot be implemented without expenditure on various social sectors by the state.

The dichotomy between these two groups of rights based on resources is untenable. The expenditure of resources is warranted for all rights. The effective realization of rights is impossible in the absence of costs. Enforceability, which is a condition of right being a right, or a genuine right, is going to involve costs and those costs are going to involve questions of justice and fairness in the distribution of the resources necessary to enforce rights. So if the enforceability is a necessary condition for a right being a right, then all rights necessarily involve the costs of enforcement.[42]

If enforceability is an essential feature of rights including negative rights, then this, of necessity, is going to involve resources in that it is not feasible to think of enforceability as costless. If this is so, then enforceability cost is not, as it were, contingent conditions for the protection of rights but are logical structure of rights claims. Thus the arguments of resource allocation and its problem apply to negative rights and the enforceability as much as they do to positive rights.[43] The allocation of resources depends upon policy and politics of a given society. The discretion of the government to allocate required resources should not take away the feature of rights. Inadequate allocation of resources in enforcement of socio-economic rights will be as detrimental as in civil and political rights.

The reality is that full realization of civil and political rights is heavily dependent both on the availability of resources and the development of the necessary societal structures. The suggestion that realization of civil and political rights requires only abstention on the part of the State and can be achieved without significant expenditure is patently at odds with reality.[44]

However it has been argued that what matters is not the quantity of government expenditure but the type of government action required and the aims pursued. Further, there is a marked difference between the expenditure to avoid inhuman and degrading treatment on the one hand and expenditure to realize an economic right on the other. The state does not initially engage in building prisons in order to protect the human rights of prisoners. The state builds prisons, establishes a police force and so forth in order to create the public good of order and security and to protect rights to integrity of person and property. The establishment of prisons, police force and judicial institution for effective realization of civil and political rights is indispensable for *complete enforcement* of these rights. Civil and political rights warrants state to spend for establishing other institutions for their protection and promotion.

The distinction does not therefore depend upon the fact of government expenditure. Since all governmental activity costs money, a claim that civil and political rights can be implemented cost free is equivalent to a claim that there should be no government. Nor does the distinction depend upon the amount of money spent. There is no magic figure, whether in absolute terms or as a percentage of GDP, that crosses the line from the implementation of one kind of right to the other. Rather the distinction is one of the quality or type of government activity.

Positive rights, if 'delivered' by government, require rationing and require the compulsory transfer of resources from one individual to another. Negative rights require only the provision of services equally available at all times to all. The argument is tenuously relating these rights on the parameters of resources. Because the socio-economic rights do not only speak about the need of deprived but also those who are having means. State is obliges to ensure protection to such individuals so that they should not be deprived of it due to action of third parties.

Indisputably, certain socio-economic rights require availability of resources for its realization. The resources may be arranged domestically or in cooperation with international agencies or nations. The International Covenant categorically speaks about the assistance of international agencies in realization of socio-economic rights.[45] The insufficient resources at the hand of the government should not be a ground of denial of status of right to socio-economic rights. Resources can be allotted looking into the need of society. Such discretion exists in civil and political rights also. In case of seditious crime, state spends more money in investigation. The existence of discretion should not negate the nature of these rights as rights.

The importance of some of the socio-economic rights requires immediate attention. Realization of such rights cannot be postponed on the basis of want of resources in the hand of state. Rights like right to adequate standard of living, right to shelter, right to education contribute effectively in meaningful exercise of other rights. The international agencies have underlined the core of obligations to be fulfilled by the state in available resources. In laying down obligations the special rapportuer, Trubek, to the Committee on ECOSOC observes that the state parties are obligated to fulfill economic, social and cultural rights regardless of the level of economic development. The states are obliged to ensure respect for minimum subsistence for all.[46]

The different kind of available resources can be channelized to implement socio-economic rights. The resources can be classified in broad terms viz., monetary, natural, human, information and technology. One of the enduring resources is money. Financial resources can be put into the hands of those in need, or can be used by the state to purchase items for the needy. However, dependence on financial resources is somewhat flawed, as it does little to promote self-reliance.[47] Material resources will be more useful to the rural people. Conferment of natural sources, ensuring land, water, animals, will make them more self-reliable. It will alleviate the problem of perpetual state dependency. Human resources in form of civil society and like will play instrumental role in taking governmental plan to people and suggest means of effective implementation of policies and programmes through their surveys and studies. Technology and information can revolutionize the realization of socio-economic rights.

The state is bound to realize the socio-economic rights within the available capacities. Available resources need to be identified meticulously to ensure effective realization of socio-economic interest of individual. There is a need to optimally pull in resources available in order to implement these rights.[48] The state cannot take the plea of non-availability of resources for fulfillment of core-obligations of the rights.

CONCLUSION

Socio-economic rights must be understood and accepted as important and inherent core of human rights. Socio-economic rights deal with well-being, decent life and physical integrity of individual. The factors such as resources, indeterminate, need-based, non-universal were advanced to relegate position of socio-economic rights on the landscape of human rights. They are, generally, considered as duties imposed upon government to implement socio-economic needs of individual rather than a right to claim those needs. They have been deprived of elementary attributes of rights.

The poverty of language of rights affected their development. Their importance as rights has been also ignored by leading civil societies. Thus it is imperative upon the advocates of socio-economic rights to clothe them in the wrap of right-based language. It has, historically, been witnessed that right based approach has strengthened the fabric of rights. It has been realized and enjoyed by generations. The progress of the State is quantified on the basis of the respect it pays to the rights. Therefore, state pledges to fulfill its obligation to enforce these rights. The court has, actively, been clarifying the meaning and the content of civil and political rights. People can of course have rights without being able to explain them – without being able to articulate the principles that apply to their cases and serve the reasons for their demand. Rights are meaningful rhetoric for discussing society's response to human needs. Rights rhetoric is more than aspiration. It is commitment of some degree of action.[49]

Rights must be made enforceable so that their implementation shouldn't be left on the sweet-will of the policy makers. Declaration of rights looses any practical meaning if there is no possibility of their effective application. The absence of enforceability can rather take away the character of rights. Rights defined as having "progressive" applicability cannot be viewed as being genuine rights. Quite correctly, Bobbio wonders whether:

> " a right whose acknowledgement and effective protection are postponed sine die in addition to being dependant on the will of subjects whose obligation to implement the "programme" may be merely a moral (or at the most political) obligation, can correctly be called a 'right'? (...) The figure of the right is correlated to the figure of the obligation."[50]

Socio-economic rights involve different methods of enforcement due to their different nature. They involve dual step: firstly, to identify entitlements – obligation based approach and secondly, enforcement of such obligation – right based approach. Enforcement of these rights deals with the identification of the entitlements and duties created by legal regime which have to be maintained and executed.

The open-ended formulations of these rights are advantageous in terms of progressing society. The content of these rights may be drawn from the prevailing situation of the society. Human rights discourse must not remain static; it is dynamic in nature and should continue to fill its content as per need and demands of the society. The specificity of rights varies according to society and circumstances prevailing in it. For instance, the level of clothing or shelter needs vary according to the climate. The efforts are made at the international level to identify 'minimum core' of various socio-economic rights.[51] The judiciary has been deducing specific rights from the general terminology of rights.[52]

All this establishes the need to reformulate the distinct concepts of Civil and Political, and Social and Economic Rights and also to reformulate the techniques of protection and promotion of one and the other. The reformulation must eliminate the separation and division between both types of rights and lead to more integrative position. All human rights, including socio-economic rights, ensure dignified and decent life to an individual. The two categories of rights must be seen in 'relational' nature; comprehensiveness of rights must be construed in relation to other rights.

Notes

1. Traer, Robert, Faith in Human Rights 216 (1991), p 10. See also, Mahendra P Singh, Human Rights in the Indian Constitution - Search for an Alternative Model, in Human Rights and Basic Needs, Mahendra P Singh, Helmut Goerlich & Michael von Hauff (eds), Universal Law Publishing, New Delhi, 2008; Surya P Subedi, Are the Principles of Human Rights "Western" Ideas? A Analysis of the Claims of the "Asian" Concept of Human Rights from the Perspectives of Hinduism, 30 California Western Int'l Law Journal, 45 (1999); Yogesh K Tyagi, Third World response to Human Rights, 21 Indian Journal of Int'l Law, 119 (1981); Yogindra Khushalani, Human Rights in Asia and Africa, 4 HRLJ, 403 (1983).
2. Cranston, M., What are Human Rights? The Bodley Head, London,1973, p 67, where he Cranston identifies three characteristics of human rights as international moral rights: they must be universal, fundamental, and practicable.
3. Cranston, supra, n 2, at 49-51.
4. Article 11.1 of the Universal Declaration of Human Rights.
5. Sieghart, P., The Lawful Rights of Mankind,1985, p. 158.
6. For instance, the controversial artistic work of M F Hussein was seen in conflict with right of religious feelings of others.

7. Waldron, J., Rights in Conflict, *Ethics*, 99 (1989), 503-19, 503.
8. See, For elaborative reference, Berlin, I., Two Concepts of Liberty, (1958), he has made the distinction on the line of negative and positive freedom.
9. See, S Freedman, "Social, Economic and Cultural Rights" in D Feldman, ed., English Public Law, Oxford University Press, 2004.
10. Reference may be drawn from various judicial pronouncements of Indian Supreme Court and South African Constitutional Court.
11. Shue, H., Basic Rights: Subsistence, Affluence and US Foreign Policy, 2nd Ed., Princeton Univeristy Press, Princeton, 1996 p. 52.
12. See, The Right to Food as a Human Rights, 7 July 1987, E/CN. 4/ Sub.2/1987/23.
13. Eide, *Realization of Social and Economic Rights and the Minimum Threshold Approach*, (1989) 10 HRLJ, 35.
14. Kunnemann, Rolf., *A Coherent Approach to Human Rights*, 17 Hum. Rts Q 323 (1995), 328.
15. General Comments No. 3, UN Doc. E/1991/23.
16. General Comments No. 4. UN Doc E/1992/23, para 17.
17. Certification of the Constitution of the Republic of South Africa, 1996 (4) SA 744 (CC) para 78.
18. Macklem, Timothy, *Entrenching Bill of Rights*, OJLS 2006 26 (107).
19. See, van Hoof, The Legal Nature of Economic, Social and Cultural Rights: A rebuttal of Some Traditional Views, in The Right to Food, Alston and Tomasevski (eds). p. 106.
20. Steiner and Alston, International Human Rights in Context, 2nd edn., Oxford University Press, Oxford, 2000, p. 182.
21. See, Sepu Iveda, The Nature of the Obligations under the International Covenant on Economic, Social and Cultural Rights, Hart Publications, Oxford, 2003 at Chapters IV and V.
22. Part IV A of the Constitution of India–Fundamental Duties Incorporated through 42nd Constitutional Amendment Act, 1976.
23. The difference can be observed by analyzing 'will theory' propounded by HLA Hart and 'Interest Theory' propounded by Joseph Raz. The former views it as protection of individual assertion and waivable whereas later views it as protection of certain interest and cannot be waived.
24. See, d'Entreves, A., Natural Law: An Introduction to Legal Philosophy (1970), pp. 51-63.
25. See, Eide, A., Realization of Social and Economic Rights and the Minimum Threshold Approach, Human Rights in the World Community, eds., Richard Pierre Claude & Burns Weston, 1992, 158-159.

26. See, Schutter de Olivier, The Protection of Social Rights in Europe, Social, Economic and Cultural Rights: An appraisal of Current European and International Developments, Peter Van der Auwerwert *et al.* eds., 2002, 207, 232.

27. Tomasevski, K., *Justiciability of Economic, Social and Cultural Rights*, 55 The Review Int'l Comm'n Jurists, Dec. 1995, 203, 217.

28. Preuz, U K., The Conceptual Difficulties of Welfare Rights, in Western Rights? Post-Communist Application, Andras Sajo (ed.), Kluwer Law International, Netherlands, 1996, p. 211.

29. Robertson, R., The Right to Food in International Law, in Human Rights in the Twenty-First Century: A Global Challenge, Kathleen E Mahoney & Paul Mahoney (eds.), 1993, 451 at 453.

30. See, ECOSOC, Comm. On Econ., Soc. & Cultural Rts., Substantive Issues Arising in the Implementation of the International Covenant on Economic, Social and Cultural Rights: General Comment 12: The Right to Adequate Food, P. 19, 6 UN Doc E/C.12/1999/5 (May 12, 1999) giving examples where a right to adequate food would have been violated, including: "repeal or suspension of legislation necessary for the continued enjoyment of the right to food; denial of access to food to particular individuals or groups, whether the discrimination is based on legislation or is proactive; (and) the prevention of access to humanitarian food aid in internal conflicts or other emergency situation").

31. Liebenberg, S., Social and Economic Rights, M. Chaskalson *et al*, eds., Constitutional Law of South Africa, Cape Town, 1996, 41-51.

32. Alston, P., *Making Economic and Social Rights Count: A Strategy for the Future*, The Political Quarterly, 1997, 188-195, 191.

33. Article 12(2)(b) ICESCR.

34. Article 12(2)(c) ICESCR.

35. In India, the right to education is related to primary education, from the age of 6 to 14.

36. 19(2) of the Constitution of India deals with reasonable restrictions on freedom of speech and expression.

37. State of Madhya Pradesh v. Pramod Bhartiya, AIR 1993 SC 286.

38. Vishaka v State of Rajasthan, AIR 1997 SC 3011

39. Sodan Singh v NDMC, AIR 1992 SC 1153

40. Beck, G., *The Idea of Human Rights Between Value Pluralism and Conceptual Vagueness*, 25 Penn St. Int'l L Rev. 615, 620.

41. *Ibid.* at 626.

42. Plant, R., Social and Economic Rights Revisited, (2003) 14 KCLJ 1-20, p. 11.
43. *Ibid.* at 12.
44. Alston & Quinn, *The Nature and Scope of State Parties' Obligations under the International Covenant on Economic, Social and Cultural Rights*, (1987) 8 Hum. Rts Q 156, 172.
45. Article 2 (1) of ICESCR
46. The New International Economic Order and the Promotion of Human Rights: Realization of Economic, Social and Cultural Rights; Progress Report Prepared by Danilo Turk, UN Commission on Human Rights, Sub-Commission on Prevention of Discrimination and Protection of Minorities, 42nd Sess., Provisional Agenda Item 7 at 18, UN Doc. E/CN.4/Sub.2/1991/17.
47. Robertson, E R., *Measuring State Compliance with the Obligation to Devote the "Maximum Available Resources" to realizing Economic, Social and Cultural Rights*, 16 Hum. Rts. Q. (1994) 693, 695.
48. Committee on Economic, Social and Cultural Rights, Report on the Fifth Session, UN ESCOR, Supp. No. 3 at 86, para 9 UN Doc. No. E/C 12/1990/8 (1990).
49. See, Economic and Social Rights and the Right to Health, Harvard Law School Human Rights Programme, 1995.
50. Bobbio, N., 'Direitos do Homem e Sociedade', in : A Era dos Direitos, Rio De Janerios (editora campus), 1992, p. 79-80, as cited in Indivisibility and Enforceability, Lima Jr. J. B., Dignity and Human Rights The Implementation of Economic, Social and Cultural Rights, (ed.), Intersentia, p. 53.
51. See, e.g., Maastricht Guidelines on Violations of Economic, Social and Cultural Rights, adopted 22-26 Jan. 1997, reprinted in the Maastricht Guidelines on Violations of Economic, Social, and Cultural Rights, 20 Hum. Rts. Q. 691 (1998); the Limburg Principles on the Implementation of Economic, Social and Cultural Rights, adopted 8 Jan. 1987, UN ESCOR, Comm'n on Human Rights, 43rd Sess., Agenda Item 8, UN Doc. E/CN.4/1987/17/Annex (1987), reprinted in the Limburg Principles on the Implementation of the Economic, Social, and Cultural Rights, 9 Hum. Rts. Q. 122 (1987); Draft Guidelines: A Human Rights Approach to Poverty Reduction Strategies, adopted 10 Oct. 2002 UN OHCHR.
52. See for instance, the Supreme Court of India gives purposive interpretation to the right to life under article 21 of the Constitution of India to include various social and economic rights like, right to health, right to shelter, right to education etc..

Virtues, Perfectionism and Natural Law

Michele Mangini*

PREMISE

Liberalism is weak from the point of view of value orientation, many contend, because it neglects that central part of human experience expressed by substantive ideas of the good, such as human flourishing, the good life, human goodness, etc. In this paper, we argue, there is a long tradition in Western culture of a substantive view of human goodness revolving around the *virtues*. This tradition is supportive of, and still belongs to, liberal political theory insofar as we want to accept the assumption that the cultural (especially ethical) presuppositions of liberalism are embodied (at least partly) within *natural law*. The work of retrieval and analysis necessary to forwarding our argument will found a few claims concerning the compatibility between the ethical core of the virtues and liberalism. The substantive proposal of human goodness we put forward, named *agency goods perfectionism*, is an attempt at continuity between a *morality* based on the virtues, in agreement with natural law tradition, and a *political morality* in which liberal pluralism is balanced by some degree of value orientation through 'general and vague' conceptions of the virtues. The argument is developed with the aim of showing more overlapping than that usually accepted between a secular political theory, such as liberalism, and a religiously inspired conception, such as natural law. In order to put forward our argument, we shall challenge, in the course of this paper, some competing substantive ethical

* *Associate Professor, Political Philosophy, University of Bari, Italy.*

theories, such as objective list theories and new natural law theory, also aimed at addressing the problem of value-orientation but which, in our view, from directions threatening the fundamental liberal presuppositions of freedom of choice. We shall follow a sort of chronological path of inquiry starting from the revival of the ethics of virtues in the last decades and developing, on the one hand, toward one of the most plausible contemporary theories of the good, perfectionism. On the other, we shall carefully consider classical natural law theory whose ethical core, we assume, is a conception of the virtues that promises to dovetail nicely with a liberal perfectionism.

VIRTUE ETHICS AND ITS LEGACY

In recent decades ethical theory has known a revival of interest in the traditional concept of the 'virtues'. If the pioneer attempt at criticizing modern moral philosophy dates back to five decades ago,[1] it is in the last quarter of a century that a plethora of works on the virtues has infused new lymph into contemporary moral debate.[2] The general trend of the ethics of virtues (EV) is characterized by dissatisfaction with some of the main features of modern moralities (basically utilitarianism and Kantianism). They are charged with (1) being act-oriented rather than agent-oriented, taking the act and its consequences as the central object of evaluation rather than the agent and his traits of character. A welcome consequence of virtue ethics is its attention on moral excellences and admirable characters, such as moral heroes and saints. Virtue ethics has the merit of focussing on the psychology and motivations of morally excellent characters;[3] (2) interpreting moral motivation in an indirect way: for the Kantian deontologist the moral motive is the concept of duty and for the utilitarian it is the goal of utility-maximization rather than exercising a certain virtue for its own sake.[4] The indirect interpretation leads to the subordination of the virtues to other moral concepts. Influential theorists such as Philippa Foot argue that the virtues are characteristics beneficial for one's own sake and for one's fellows. The central concept is surely that of wellbeing rather than that of the virtues.[5] On another view, the virtues are correctives for the baser human impulses and motives. On such a view, "a moral virtue is a character trait which produces good consequences for others."[6] It is a consequentialist view according to which the virtues are "necessary for successful social interaction."[7] Famously, it was Hume who advocated the instrumentalist view of the virtues which inspires so many theorists of utilitarian inclination; (3) they are charged with being universalist moralities paying little or no attention to the *particularity* of the ethical situation and its circumstances. Virtue ethics often contrasts its context sensitive reading of the moral situation which can encompass a large number of ethically salient features with universalist moralities which evaluate an act as detached from its context. Furthermore, the virtues are held to allow a 'particularist' understanding and evaluation of the moral situation which goes through the *emotions*. These are an essential constituent of value, especially in the case of interpersonal relations. Emotions also provide evaluative practical knowledge of what is ethically salient and direct our attention and action towards what is most valuable.[8] (4) Virtue theories are also charged with not being clearly aligned on the line of ethical objectivism but with often being characterized by some degree of relativism. MacIntyre's account in *After Virtue*[9] is most renowned in connecting the virtues to social practices and traditions but is surely not alone. Other theorists emphasize that a certain set of habits, skills or dispositions qualify as virtues when admired or deemed beneficial, sometimes even as a cultural ideal. On this view, the virtues may be variable in number and content, according, at least, to age and role of the agent and his socio-economic context.[10] (5) Lastly, modern moral theories are charged with reserving only a marginal position for the theory of the good.[11] (We shall expand on this point in the course of this paper)[12].

This very short and incomplete outline provides some suggestions regarding the issues that virtue ethics has introduced in the moral debate. The debate has surely been reinvigorated but one large issue is still largely neglected and deserves attention in this paper: the relationship between virtues and human flourishing. Such a relationship was strong and widely accepted in ancient Greek ethics but weakened in later centuries and tends to be neglected in the modern age. On the one hand, a part of Christian ethics taught a morality of duty, understanding duty in terms of acts complying with law. Catholic moralists in particular were preoccupied with specific acts as possible sins, so virtues held only a secondary position with regard to laws and rules. On the other hand, at the beginning of the seventeenth century natural law thinking seems to steer decidedly towards rule ethics. One of its main advocates, Hugo Grotius, convincingly rejected the central aspects of Aristotelian virtue ethics, among which the privileged status of insight in the virtuous agent.[13]

On my view, the historical antecedents explain not only the general 'neglect of the virtues' but also the sharp separation between moral theory and the concept of human flourishing or wellbeing which haunts contemporary ethics. If the virtues of the ancient tradition characterized an ethics in which moral and prudential aspects - i.e. concerning human flourishing and wellbeing - were fused in one single outlook, by contrast the contemporary revival of virtue ethics has set aside, with few exceptions, the view of the virtues as a conception of human flourishing.[14] By contrast, what brings together virtue theorists such as Wiggins, McDowell, Richardson, Sherman and Nussbaum, are at least beliefs regarding the plurality and qualitative heterogeneity of the good; the centrality of reason in choosing not only means to ends but also in deliberating about the ends themselves; emotion and desire as complex forms of intentionality that can be shaped by reasoning about the good. These few suggestions shed light on the real complexity of the virtues when looked at through a conception of human flourishing in which reason, deliberation, emotion and desire have their proper place.[15] In contemporary views, considerations on human flourishing are either translated in terms of wellbeing, with all its utilitarian and subjectivist implications, or left to 'marginal' views, such as perfectionism and natural law theory. The main views of liberal political theory, such as contractualism and utilitarianism, rely on a weak or minimal theory of the good which is of little or no help to individual reflection on the classical Socratic question 'how should one live?'. No help can come to individuals who search for orientation in making major life choices. Nor is this weakness more helpful when the state has to take a substantial position on some public policy.

At least two main negative consequences of the weakness of the good can be identified. Firstly, at a political level, orthodox Kantian liberals found human rights on the idea of respect for persons and this, in turn, on free agency and the idea of people as ends in themselves while forgetting those claims for self-realization, excellence and the common good which belong to the public life as much as to the private. Secondly, at the ethical level of individual reflection, the Western world is only apparently afflicted by a general disorientation concerning what is valuable and good in human life. Liberalism is always taken as a pluralistic political theory offering each and every citizen the possibility of choosing among a large variety of heterogeneous values – often mutually incompatible. It often goes unnoticed that beneath such a large variety hides a unique model of individual value and success which pervades most individual choices in Western society. Contemporary signs of success, such as acquisition of material goods and exhibition of status symbols, have a special appeal to individual desire and reason since urged by social communication and culture in a consumerist society. Thus, we have a special need of an ideal of human flourishing which allows a 'critical potential' over existing social ideas about the good: this is the underlying *ratio* of our perfectionist proposal in the coming sections.

In the face of this theoretical and hermeneutical background this paper aims to propose two main claims: (1) contemporary virtue ethics has largely downplayed the real potential of the virtues for morality; (2) perfectionism and natural law theory have much to offer contemporary moral and political debate and the best results can be expected when their focus converges on the virtues. The second claim entails the need to tackle in parallel two ethical trends which have been kept separate: perfectionism as a marginal view within liberal theory and natural law theory as a dominion of Christian ethics. We propose there is a strong connection and a large area of overlapping between these two theoretical approaches. One influential reason for this continuity of ideas depends on their being the legitimate heirs of two major thinkers of the past having much in common: Aristotle and Aquinas. While the former is the recognized father of most perfectionist views, the latter represents the inevitable reference point for most contemporary natural law theories. Given the well-known influence of Aristotle on Aquinas's ethics, it is plausible to think that their contemporary heirs can be more in agreement than is usually acknowledged. Historical continuities establish at least a legitimate suspicion of agreement between two areas of ethical thought. If established, this agreement would, on the one hand, induce both perfectionists and natural law theorists to take their mutual claims seriously and seek a common ground to address political issues. On the other hand, their mutual interaction and debate may generate improvements in their arguments against the dominant minimalism of the good. In turn, the latter has only to gain from well-founded criticisms from the opposite camp.

However, the alleged agreement between perfectionism and natural law theory can work theoretically and have practical effects only if, after a careful review of the field, we shall be able to establish that the best views, both for perfectionism and natural law theory, are synthesised in a certain conception of human flourishing constituted primarily by the virtues. In order to reach this conclusion we need to tackle and dismiss those views in which such a conception has no place.

What is at stake in arguing for the alliance of perfectionism and natural law theory? Liberalism offers a political morality that, in mainstream versions such as Rawls's, has been charged with being discontinuous from individual ethics,[16] while perfectionism and natural law theory argue for the necessary continuity between politics and ethics: if some more or less vague idea of individual flourishing can be recognized, the state has to take it into account. In a nutshell, this is the idea, rejected by dominant liberal views, fearing continuity between politics and ethics as a potential source of restrictions on the plurality of values. By contrast, I am quite persuaded that developing an argument in favour of an alliance between perfectionism and natural law can improve their position within morality and also represent a stimulus towards a better understanding of the theory of the good within liberal political morality. In detail, it may be rewarding for a variety of reasons: (a) the alliance may offer Western people a plausible key of ethical orientation by pressing on the overlapping consensus of secular and religious (Christian) views;[17] (b) the alliance may help to establish where liberalism stands, once accepted there being more to it than mere 'rights talk' and that the vocabulary of the virtues is an unavoidable substrate of ethical practices (sect. 2); (c) the analysis of perfectionism necessary to establish the alliance (sect. 3) will help to make clarity along the way within a contemporary theory of the good in which (I) objective list theories misguide our understanding of perfectionism, (sect. 4) (II) a certain interpretation of virtue ethics as a conception of human flourishing offers an acceptable perfectionist view, largely overlapping the gist of natural law theory, (sect. 5) (III) natural law theory deserves re-evaluation from a liberal point of view, because its substantive content may overlap a liberal perfectionist view to a large degree (sect. 6-7).

Liberal 'Rights Talk'

A series of important and substantial issues have been proposed for discussion in the previous section but we cannot but start from 'rights talk' in this one. The language of rights is so widely spread and used that any proposal of alliance between liberal and natural law (NL) views is to be initially justified against the background of rights. If we want to take the ethics of virtues (EV) as a plausible ground for an alliance between the main contemporary normative (political and moral) theories of the good, we should firstly reject the plausible objection that the alliance between liberal and natural law theory is already established and framed in terms of (human or fundamental) rights which express all that moral substance of human dignity, equality of respect, individual freedom, etc. that is at the core of both doctrines. In order to contemplate the whole issue and take aboard the new language of virtues, we should have very serious and plausible motives. So, in this section our task is to verify how the language of rights has been gradually losing a part of its overall strength and persuasiveness after an honourable birth.

It is commonly acknowledged that the modern doctrine of natural rights derived from a more ancient idea of 'objective rights', as claims arising out of an objective moral order. Perhaps, we can better grasp the true content of objective rights, referring to the Roman concept of *jus*. This is taken primarily as 'the just thing itself' or 'the what is fair': it includes not only what a beneficiary has a right to in a just relationship but also the duties and obligations deriving from it.[18] So, the idea of *jus* is quite representative of the ancient doctrine of NL in which the interior power of moral discernment corresponds to the order pervading the whole universe, whereas the modern idea, found in an embryonic form in some scholastic authors, transforms a natural right into a person's power or ability which he may elect to exercise or not. It defines a sphere of liberty where the individual is free to act as he sees fit.[19] This is not to say there is no balance between rights and duties in the modern conception but only to emphasize that, whereas the ancient conception sought harmony between individual rights and objective moral order, in modern minds the individual right finds its boundary in the duties of others.

If readers remain unpersuaded by the historical thesis that places the roots of the subjective modern notion of natural rights in the XIII century, with the Scholastics, one can safely assume that the watershed is crossed at the beginning of the XVII century with Suarez and Grotius. Both focus on the idea of natural rights as moral qualities of the person, dropping most of the ancient objective idea which was dominant only about three centuries earlier. According to the modern notion, the *jus naturale* gives a person the power to advance his moral claims against other persons or the community. In a nutshell, we might express the 'decisive shift' Tierney identifies in the idea of *jus naturale* in the transformed relationships between individual and community. Whereas the classical *jus naturale* described the harmonious position of the individual within a universal moral order and, so, also within his community, the modern *jus naturale* offers each individual the necessary ethical tools to oppose his own community, to stand out and declare his difference from the community to which he belongs.

If we now pass from early XIII century to contemporary times, we find a successful example of overlapping consensus in the doctrine of *human rights* which is both the heir of theologically loaded natural rights and a result of the moral progress of the Enlightenment. If Tierney's analysis is correct, the scholastic account of the human person as a free and self-determining agent prepared a theological ground for the secular development of the Enlightenment. Contemporary rights discourse offers various attractive lists of universal rights which should compel acceptance by any rational person. An impressive international consensus has gathered around the doctrine of human rights (including both negative and positive rights), especially after the Second World War.

So far, this constitutes the bright side of the rights doctrine. However, looking a little closer, a few dark spots seem to emerge. Firstly, on the international level, a very broad agreement on general definitions, such as a right to human dignity, may not be coupled by agreement when, for example, that right is spelled out as the right of a woman to marry the spouse of her choice.[20] Secondly, disagreement on rights may go further if we consider some religious doctrine or ethnic group which tends to deny foundations of the human rights doctrine, such as equality between men and women.[21] Legal declarations may strengthen the language of rights (although with some heterogeneity of meanings), but they still clash with contradictory or conflicting practices in many areas of the world. The universalistic power of human rights is put to the question here and shall be taken up later when examining natural law theory.

In order to reach a clear understanding of the true meaning and position of human rights in contemporary society we should try to shed some light on their controversial aspects which are pervasive and problematic for Western culture, before taking into account_any multicultural complication. The general complaint is that rights are individualistic, and set each person apart from others. Each person is brought to see himself as an island to be defended against the intrusion of others or the state. This complaint is usually made by those wishing to promote the common good against "atomistic" rights. It can be called the 'communitarian complaint'. Another complaint is that rights are intransigent. They do not leave room for compromise but lead straight to conflict since each right is a 'political trump', an absolute claim. A right is self-assertive and cannot be traded off against other claims. Nor does rights-talk lead to solidaristic solutions to our political and social problems. We can call it the 'solidarity complaint'. Lastly, critics complain that ceaseless appeal to rights will reduce their effectiveness through a sort of conceptual inflation. If everyone claims to have rights to everything, no-one will have effective rights to anything. This is the 'inflation complaint'.[22]

This set of complaints focuses on the place of rights within political morality and attacks the inadequacy of rights-talk within the political vocabulary, determined by gaps shown from several perspectives. We shall now consider a general attack to rights-based moralities as impoverished moralities which, in their language of rights and correlative duties, cannot take into account other important moral concepts such as supererogation and the pursuit of excellences. Joseph Raz holds that supererogatory acts are praiseworthy, though not morally wrong to omit them. Since there is no right that another person acts in a supererogatory way, right-based moralities cannot account for the nature of supererogation. Similarly, the pursuit of excellence and the exercise of virtues – usually taken as a particular kind of excellences – cannot be understood in terms of respect for rights. For example, the person of courage is led to acts, motives and an emotional commitment which no duty could explain. Right-based moralities cannot give their true moral significance to these concepts.[23]

The problem between right-based moralities and virtues is not that the former have no place for the latter, rather that the former can conceive of virtues only as instrumentally valuable. Virtues cannot be taken as morally praiseworthy characteristics to be cultivated for their own sake, although right-based and utilitarian theories may take them as instrumental in predisposing individuals, respectively, to do their duty or maximize utility. Raz stresses that a right-based morality, taken essentially as a morality of rights and duties, does not have conceptual space for the virtues. However, this point does not exclude the possibility that a liberal *political* morality based on rights be balanced by a general morality which allows an understanding of the intrinsic value of the virtues.

A further set of complaints against prevailing 'rights-talk' comes from different quarters: communitarians, republicans and natural law theorists charge rights-based moralities with neglecting the common good. It is not so much a utilitarian conception of the common welfare at stake here (rather the conception of 'general welfare' has always been a target for rights-theorists), as is a NL conception of the common good as a synthesis of the various aspects of individual wellbeing of all citizens of a community. As Finnis correctly comments, even the Universal Declaration of Human Rights of 1948 expresses a few general limitations to the exercise of individual rights, limitations such as security for the rights of others, the requirements of morality in a democratic society and the requirements of public order. These limitations express more than those duties toward individual others which are correlative of rights and as much universally held. Rather, these limitations express the richer and more complex concept of 'the common good'.[24] Thus, what is most interesting for our purposes is that the list of rights of the Universal Declaration (including many 'social rights', such as rest and leisure [art. 24] or enjoyment of the arts [art. 27]) is "simply a way of sketching the outlines of the common good, the various aspects of individual wellbeing in a community."[25] Framed in these terms, the view of rights expressed in the Declaration comes closer to overlapping the idea of the common good than many liberal individualistic conceptions.

Finnis's argument clearly unveils what sometimes remains concealed in many contemporary rights theories: there is no point in rights without their *ratio* in human wellbeing.[26] This explains better and more convincingly than any foundation on overlapping consensus why we can detect certain recurring aspects of moral practices which seem to cut across cultural and historical diversity. Insofar as we can read into human rights, a content which goes beyond the expression of local traditions and mores, we can think of the language of rights as a supple tool to respond effectively to recurrent needs. However, taking rights as simple expressions of basic needs would be too reductivist and inadequate to explain the *ratio* of many contemporary rights. We can also identify at least two main *universalist* roots behind recurrences in human rights: human dignity and the development of human potentialities. If taken seriously, these 'roots' show there is more to 'rights talk' than what most rights theorists care to admit. We may even notice that once we start looking for a *ratio* of 'what is right or wrong to do', *sic et simpliciter* we move beyond 'rights talk'.

If we accept the appeal of these two 'meta-goods' as ultimate grounds for human rights, as what justifies their weight and importance in contemporary moral theory, we have a strong justification to inquire into perfectionism as a serious contender with rights theories for establishing an alliance with NL theory. However, in discussing perfectionism in general we would have performed only half of our task. The other half consists in explaining if perfectionism can be interwoven with some kind of EV. In order to achieve our goal we need (1) a general understanding of what a perfectionist theory is (sect. 3), (2) a discussion of some influential contemporary perfectionist theory which sheds light on their eventual weaknesses (sect. 3.1, 4, 4.1) and, lastly, (3) the proposal of a perfectionist view in which EV plays a crucial role (sect. 5, 5.1).

DIFFERENT BRANDS OF PERFECTIONISM

The path of inquiry we are following leads us to tackle one of the main contenders in the contemporary moral landscape which gives pride of place to the theory of the good. Therefore, we are not discussing, mainstream liberal theory, such as Rawls's, Dworkin's or Ackerman's contributions. Rather, the perfectionist theory we wish to discuss in this section has been largely neglected in contemporary liberalism, although having an ancient and respectable pedigree. Philosophers such as Aristotle, Plato, Aquinas, Spinoza, Leibniz, Kant, Hegel, Green, Bradley and Marx have been counted in the perfectionist field.[27] Among contemporary writers, Raz, Nozick,[28] Haksar, Hurka and Sher express some kind of perfectionist view.

This variety of authors, of course, bespeaks very different views about perfectionism, so where should we start in defining perfectionism in general? I believe it is useful to make clear that we are moving within the theory of the good where perfectionism has to situate itself with regard to theories of the good encapsulated in concepts such as happiness, well-being or welfare. All these concepts are broadly 'subjectivist' and are commonly used to ground liberal theories. Close distinctions between these concepts are beyond the purposes of our inquiry.[29] Suffice to say that in each of these cases the good is subjectively characterized as what is 'good for' someone because he desires it, makes him happy, or is in his interests ('happiness' implies that something is good because it brings pleasure or some other favourable state of mind, while 'well-being' or 'welfare' refer to what is beneficial for the agent; all these terms refer to what is 'good for' a person rather than good *tout court*). By contrast, perfectionism relates to what is good in human beings as such. Following the author who has contributed most to contemporary reflection on perfectionism, Thomas Hurka, we might say that the perfectionist tradition "shares the foundational idea that what is good, ultimately, is the development of human nature".[30] He discusses formal criteria at length, such as distinctiveness and essence to determine the content of human nature. He takes hints from the well-known Aristotelian discussion of the good life but only as far as Aristotle's formal criteria of human nature are concerned. As we shall see, Hurka's appeal to Aristotle is controversial and his view is not broad enough to encompass all authors who have proposed versions of perfectionism.

Therefore, taking Aristotle's ethics as the clearest discussion of perfectionism as a starting point, can we define perfectionism differently from Hurka's 'development of human nature'? Should we want to keep those various authors who do not propose the development of human nature as the ideal of their undoubtedly perfectionists theories (such as Moore, Nozick, Sher, Raz, Finnis, etc.,) within the boundaries of perfectionism, I believe a different solution needs to be found. Thus, what is the distinctive feature of perfectionism differing it from other theories? From the point of view of the debate between liberalism and its critics, it seems as if a perfectionist theory always proposes a theory of the good that offers a *critical potential grounded in the ideal of human improvement,* on subjectivist accounts of the good such as happiness, well-being or welfare. Even though subjectivist theories can provide criteria for criticizing the individual's actual desires, such as procedures of rationalization or idealization of preferences, none provides an external standard to criticize people's desires from the standpoint of human improvement. We shall propose this as a *broad definition* of perfectionism.[31]

In other words, while the subjectivist theories normally associated with liberalism offer no conceptual tool to criticize and negatively assess the agent's choices of ends, since accepting only subjectivist conceptions of the good, a perfectionist theory accepts a conception of the good in light of which it is possible to criticize the agent's choices of ends. In liberal theory such a conception of the good has an important role to play on the political level, justifying government actions that go beyond people's preferences and realize goals which were not expressly chosen by individual citizens.

How should we spell out the idea of a critical potential? An obvious answer is to equate perfectionism with an 'objectivist conception of the good', where the good stands for those substantive ends worth pursuing by human beings and holding that all conceptions of the good are either subjectivist or perfectionist.[32] On such a view, any ethical theory based on some objective conception of the good – i.e., a conception in which the good is independent from people's actual desires or preferences – can be called 'perfectionist'. A perfectionist theory can either claim to orient individual conduct and offer a political guide or simply guide political action. From a liberal point of view, perfectionism on the objectivist definition runs the risk of justifying the interference of the state in individual choices. However, we do not need to follow Hurka's objectivist definition. In fact, our wider 'broad definition' of perfectionism allows us to propose a perfectionist theory compatible with liberalism. As we shall shortly see, a 'critical potential' can be derived from grounds different from an objectivist conception of the good. In my view, the objectivist definition of perfectionism is responsible for the bad name perfectionism has for many liberals. How can we correct such a misunderstanding?

In order to argue for a perfectionism *compatible with* liberalism, first of all we need, to challenge one of the most prominent examples of contemporary perfectionist theory: Hurka's maximizing consequentialism. Hurka's perfectionist theory is long and articulated. It ranges between personal and political perfectionism. Of course we cannot examine all aspects of his theory, but only those views characterizing most of his perfectionist proposal and most relevant to our three-pronged discussion concerning EV and NL theory. These aspects can be summarized as Hurka's views on: human nature, rationality and maximizing consequentialism.

(1) Hurka is persuaded that the best account of perfectionism "must remain close to whatever motivates the idea that the human good rests somehow in human nature."[33] Further, such an account should remain reasonably close to the perfectionist tradition and "our nature as defined must seem in itself morally significant."[34] From these hints we gather Hurka's desire to remain close to mainstream perfectionist tradition: Aristotle, Kant, Aquinas and Green are among the main perfectionist authors. All used moral criteria in forming their accounts of human nature, without being committed to 'commonsense morality'.[35] However, Hurka dismisses the possibility of using moral standards to identify human essence, arguing that we do not use them to identify the essences of non-human kinds. So we seem to be left with an ambivalent attitude of Hurka's perfectionism toward morality. On the one hand, perfectionism relies on human nature and this is morally significant. On the other, Hurka wishes to avoid recourse to moral criteria – a few pages later – probably for the same reasons that lead many contemporary authors to ground ethics in some objective, non-ethical naturalism. This move is perfectly plausible though it does open a gap with the perfectionist tradition and should be discussed and justified. He argues that moralism in the

perfectionist tradition is a falsehood since holding implausible claims about human nature. For example, it is absurd to claim that perfectionism should develop *distinctive* human properties because these are what distinguish humans from other beings. Hurka contests that many properties are distinctive of human beings, such as killing for fun or despoiling the environment: a perfectionism based on distinctiveness should develop these properties as intrinsically good.[36] However, in support of the perfectionist tradition one could reply that Hurka reaches these absurd conclusions because he does not appreciate that categories such as 'distinctiveness' and 'human nature' are evaluative from the start in historical perfectionists and do not commit them to thinking that all that is distinctive is also intrinsically good.

Somewhere a perfectionist author who wants to connect perfectionism to human nature and select what counts in human nature on the grounds of essence has to draw the line. It makes little sense to say that the best perfectionism depends on essential properties of human nature, although we do not yet know what properties are essential.[37] Stocker's criticisms of Hurka's view on human nature are in line with tradition. Aristotle, the foremost perfectionist thinker to whom Hurka often appeals, notoriously builds his theory from a strong and substantive conception of the good life (*eudaimonia*). His views on formal properties, such as distinctiveness , essence but also completeness, self-sufficiency and finality cannot be disconnected from his overall conception of *eudaimonia* but, can rather be understood only in light of it. Distinctiveness, to take one, cannot be taken seriously, according to Hurka, because also cruelty distinguishes human beings from other living beings. However, this is true only if one wishes to miss the point of an inquiry which is aimed at a specifically human life. Aristotle wishes to define a good human life for people who live in society with their fellows: this point of departure automatically drives out certain human features that, though unique to human beings, it is not *desirable* to develop in human nature.

If we wish to define perfectionism as a moral theory, it seems we cannot help using evaluative categories in identifying human nature. Hurka's aim to found his theory on a 'neutral naturalism' seems a hopeless task because it cannot yield more than that contained in its premises. It is difficult to conceive of Hurka's perfectionism as a moral theory, once one keeps in mind his harsh charges against the traditional perfectionism of Aristotle or Aquinas as embodying a falsehood insofar as it embodies moralistic views. A leading idea in Hurka's critique of moralistic perfectionism is that it is reduced to a popular notion of morality, not an alternative and distinctive theory (according to Sidgwick, perfectionism through the exercise of the virtues is no more than an intuitionist morality and, as such does not deserve separate discussion).[38]

(2) A second step in reviewing Hurka's perfectionist proposal needs to take up an aspect which we have as yet left open: the content of his essentialist approach and his emphasis on rationality. Hurka declares to follow Aristotle in proposing a tripartite view of perfectionism: physical perfection, practical and theoretical perfection (as rationality). While Hurka affirms physical perfection is less important, practical and theoretical rationality consist in forming and acting on beliefs, intentions and plans and developing them to be more complex and inclusive.[39] The pursuit of knowledge, according to Hurka, is not only unified scientific knowledge or other 'rarefied' forms, such as theology, philosophy or physics but it can also consist in an artist's understanding of "the quirks and capacities of his materials".[40] Notwithstanding these hints, critics such as Stocker comment that Hurka overrates abstract general thought and underrates more particular and concrete forms of thought.[41] My feeling is that Hurka's overall treatment of perfection as rationality is spoiled by his analytical method of isolating and discussing each factor on its own, detached from the whole to which it belongs.

This is typically shown by Hurka's – consequentialist – emphasis on perfectionist *measurement*. This takes place along two dimensions, number and quality: "a person's perfection will depend both on the number of states of some kind she has and on their standing on a scale of quality."[42] The idea of focusing on rationality as knowledge seems to equate perfecting people with becoming better thinkers, while leaving aside the core of Aristotelian perfectionism: the ideal of *eudaimonia* is not realized through quantitative development that can be measured in terms of rationality (number and quality of states), but consists of practical reasoning which is good because it deals with human activities, concerns and interests. So, from an Aristotelian standpoint, Hurka is surely wrong in detaching rationality from good activities and concerns that are the gist of the good life. Further, the consequentialist inclination to measurement runs in the face of the Aristotelian caution that one's reasons, goals and emotions have to be in accord with the *orthos logos* which is the opposite of a formal and sharp rule. Once again, in conclusion, Hurka's approach shows a weakness that depends on rejecting evaluative considerations in shaping his perfectionism.

(3) Our critical reading of Hurka's views stands so far, and will also be useful in reaching the next wider stage of discussion in which we shall confront Hurka's version with other possibilities within perfectionism. In my view, his emphasis on maximization qualifies his brand of perfectionism as incompatible with classical, virtue-based, perfectionism. In order to reach the next stage we need to tackle one last important aspect of his theory: its being a *maximizing consequentialism*.[43] Each of these terms requires attention and analysis because they characterize Hurka's theory in a peculiar way. Firstly, we address consequentialism. As well-known, this is one of the main components of all utilitarian theories. It states that the right action is that which produces the most good consequences. So, it gives us two relevant pieces of information: (a) the concept of the good is prior to the right and (b) the good is something to be *produced* in terms of good consequences. Therefore, what changes between a utilitarian consequentialism and a perfectionist consequentialism is only the kind of good: from utility to some kind of intrinsic goodness, such as rationality. Hurka's perfectionist consequentialism - in accordance with Rawls' understanding of perfectionism as production (maximization) of scientific and artistic excellences - holds that the good of perfection is a state of affairs to be produced. I am very doubtful Aristotle would subscribe to this understanding of perfectionism, notwithstanding Hurka's appeal to his authority. I suspect at least two general features of *eudaimonia* conflict with Hurka's consequentalism: firstly, it is an ideal consisting of a peculiar balance among different components and such a balance can be peculiarly created and developed by each agent on her own, it cannot be produced as scientific knowledge can be.[44] It is quite clear that if someone wishes to seriously take the idea of *eudaimonia* as the exercise of moral virtues requiring

special attention to salient ethical features of each situation and emotional participation, 'producing perfection' makes little sense. Secondly, consequentialism works smoothly as long as it deals with 'simple' values such as utility or preference-satisfaction which in some sense we can produce in ourselves and in others. However, when we deal with relational vales such as *friendship*, its peculiar features, namely mutual loyalty and concern, spending some time together, sharing experiences and showing sensitiveness towards the emotional states of others, they show a special dimension of value which is alive and true only for those involved, that is friends.

These considerations lead us to another central aspect of Hurka's perfectionism: its being a *maximizing* theory. He makes a controversial connection with historical tradition: "perfectionism has always been a *maximizing* morality. [...] Aristotle, for example, thinks there is a better part of the soul and wants us to strain every nerve to develop it."[45] How Aristotelian perfectionism, based on concepts such as *eudaimonia* and the virtues, can appear to Hurka's eyes as a maximizing morality is quite mysterious. As widely accepted, the virtues are excellences of character (or theoretical excellences) which consist in appropriate answers in certain spheres of human experience and do not lend themselves to maximization.[46] The case of friendship may be particularly relevant for our purposes. Friendship, as a prudential good, offers a clear example of a good whose structure is not only unconducive to maximization but whose value would be discarded by the application of maximizing rationality. The value of friendship consists in being loyal to one's friends, being concerned for them, spending time with them, etc. All these reasons imply a commitment toward certain particular persons, depending on their character and on the bonds that develop between them and the agent. When one acts as a friend he never acts to maximize the amount or value of friendship in his life or his number of friends, unless he sees friendship just as a means to desire satisfaction or pleasure.[47] None of the reasons for which people must act if they are to sustain friendship lends itself to maximization. Maximization seems misplaced not only when we take friendship as a means to pleasure but also when we take it as a final good – as Hurka would.

Friendship is a relational good which is born and cultivated within a face-to-face relationship: it does not make sense to claim to maximize its quantity in the world. The structure of friendship consists in a unique and unrepeatable personal relation that cannot be replicated or improved toward maximization. A maximizing value can be increased by the addition of more units but friendship cannot be increased by adding more affection, benevolence or other aspects. All the components of friendship are already present in a (good) friendship: it needs nothing more because its value derives from the right proportion of its components.[48] Furthermore, from the point of view of a life as a whole, it is doubtful that a search for more and more valuable friendships makes that life better. Nevertheless, from the point of view of political morality, it could be a valid perfectionist goal for a government to create and improve conditions that enable friendship to develop and last (e.g. less working hours, improving centers for social activities, etc.).

OBJECTIVE LIST THEORIES

At this point we should pause to consider that the present debate on perfectionism is the natural child of the well-known charges addressed against liberal neutrality by such authors as J. Raz and W. Galston.[49] It is the political role of the state and its eventual greater involvement in citizens' lives which is to be discussed. In this scenario Hurka's work represents an exception, covering both the personal and political aspects of perfectionism. By contrast, the range of theories we wish to compare in this section originate outwith the liberal debate, although they have been quickly employed within it, as we shall see in the case of George Sher.

'Objective list theories' (OLT), as far as I can gather, is a definition dating back to Derek Parfit's Appendix I of *Reasons and Persons*.[50] Parfit's discussion, as the title makes clear, revolves around the concept of well-being or self-interest, as Parfit himself dubs theories concerning what makes someone's life go best.[51] The outline of an objective list theory is raised against experiential theories such as hedonism and desire-fulfilment theories. According to OLT, "certain things are good or bad for people whether or not these people would want to have the good things, or to avoid the bad things. The good things might include moral goodness, rational activity, the development of one's abilities, having children and being a good parent, knowledge and the awareness of true beauty."[52]

We can agree with Parfit (and Scanlon)[53] that this list includes most desirable goods that people have always tried to pursue in their lives. However, we should also be suspicious about the effective working of such a theory as a competitor in the realm of theories of 'the good life', where the paradigm case is that of Aristotle's *eudaimonia*. Famously, Aristotle proposes a complex and interwoven ideal of how to live well and be an excellent person in which a 'list' of external goods – among which we can count 'having good children and being a good parent' – has a secondary place with regard to exercising virtuous activity and finding pleasure in it. According to Aristotle, the exercise of the virtues represents, the core of the good life, expressing both moral goodness and rational activity, that is, the two general criteria by which we can legitimately assess all people's lives because we intuitively consider a life lacking in one or the other feature as a less than human life. Whereas a life lacking in knowledge or the awareness of true beauty, as happens with a large number of human lives, is not intuitively unsuccessful because it can still be successfully evaluated on the grounds of more commonly shared features, such as moral goodness and rational activity – or, according to Aristotle's overall view of the good life, virtuous activity exercised with pleasure.[54]

So, it seems that, if we wish to locate objective list theories with regard to perfectionism, we should quite likely mark their difference in terms similar to the difference between 'how to make one's life go well' and 'living a good life'. Parfit's problem originates within subjectivist perspectives on wellbeing where the unbalance of hedonistic or desire-fulfilment theories toward subjectivism (e.g., what is good for the agent lies entirely in his sphere of experience) make it (theoretically) necessary to find a counterweight on the objective side. While an objective list theory, such as Parfit's, makes a good job in balancing subjectivist theories of wellbeing, it sits uncomfortably at the desk of perfectionist theories where the Aristotelian paradigm and its millennia-long tradition still influences the debate: a perfectionist theory suggests an ideal of the good life for persons who want to live a complete human life. In these terms it is clear that a list of disconnected, though objective, goods cannot represent a perfectionist proposal.

Sher's Argument for an Objective List Theory

After our short discussion of some of the main features of OLT we should now address a case in which the same list by Parfit has been taken up and argued for thoroughly. George Sher does not conceive of his proposal as an alternative theory of wellbeing - although he takes subjectivist theories of the good as the counterpart to his perfectionist proposal - but as a theory that stands within the liberal debate, in opposition to the principle of neutrality and its political applications.[55] While Sher offers "the most thorough critique of neutrality to date [that] will surely become the canonical one",[56] his positive proposal of a perfectionist theory is surely more controversial and deserves careful assessment.

At the outset of his work Sher wishes to give his own definition of perfectionism by drawing a sharp distinction between perfectionist and subjectivist theories of the good. His aim is to argue for a legitimate public conception of the good that the state can promote, showing concern for its citizens without interfering in their freedom to choose their own styles of life. So, Sher argues that either a theory is subjectivist because "it traces all value to some combination of actual or ideal desires, choices or enjoyments" (BN, p. 9) or it is perfectionist if it traces all value to some activities or traits which are intrinsically or inherently valuable. This definition is meant to be exhaustive and any substantive approach to value will fall into one or the other category. Sher wishes his perfectionist theory to be inclusive of views such as Rawls's artistic and scientific excellences and the view of perfection as advanced development of characteristically human capacities.[57] By contrast, Sher considers subjectivism of values the default position because each person presumably knows best his desires and cares most about their satisfaction. The idea is that any departure from subjectivism must be justified.

Although subjectivists may believe that the state should promote some traits or activities which are conducive to enjoyment or desire-satisfaction, thus violating neutrality, it is true that neutralism and subjectivism have broad affinities. Governments should not try to promote the good when all value is traced to enjoyment, desire or choice because they are very different among people and affected by a number of factors. By contrast, when some values are considered independent of enjoyment, desire and choice, it seems more legitimate for the state to promote the good. Sher's constructivist goal is to propose a list of perfectionist goods the state can act upon, independently of subjective states of individuals. One leading idea in Sher's view, as with other political perfectionists, is that governments should take an active interest in the goodness of their citizens' lives. The well-known complaint against liberalism is that it is indifferent to the quality of life of citizens.

In proposing an objective list of goods Sher considers a few alternatives but concludes that the most plausible is Parfit's list – although Parfit only introduces his proposal at the end of a very long book. Each of the goods on the list requires a specific justification connected with its own traits of goodness but the general argument that Sher introduces is that certain traits and activities are inherently valuable since associated to certain fundamental human capacities. These are described in terms of two requirements: firstly, they must be capacities that virtually all humans possess and, secondly, their exercise cannot easily be avoided. Therefore, in Sher's account, the exercise of these capacities must be near-universal and near-inescapable. However, if fundamental capacities are those virtually no one can avoid exercising, then we should conclude that virtually everyone lives a good life. (BN, p. 202) Sher avoids this implausible conclusion by insisting that what has inherent value is the *successful* exercise of fundamental capacities. We do not need to address the plausibility of each of the items on the list because no value on such lists is completely devoid of value. Rather, given our introductory remarks, we should focus on the main features of the overall picture Sher paints for his readers.

What makes Sher's perfectionist theory more important than a mere collection of objective goods, such as the list originally proposed by Parfit, is his inquiry to identify a unifying theory that explains why certain things are valuable in a coherent framework. He surveys a number of possibilities, according to two distinctions: objective/subjective (whether the source of the elements of the good life is outwith or within the subjectivity of the agent) and teleological/non teleological (whether such a source is or is not directed at a goal). We shall address Sher's option of an objective teleological theory in more detail, but the other combinations deserve quick mention at least to trace Sher's justificatory strategy.

According to Sher, a subjective non teleological theory such as hedonism locates the source of all value in pleasure or enjoyment but, in general, experiential theories have no chance of giving proper consideration to human activities, to what a person actually does in her life. In turn, an objective non teleological theory, such as Hurka's, locates the intrinsic value of traits and activities in one unifying property, such as being part of a person's essential (human) nature. So, according to Hurka, perfectionism consists in the development of human nature. Sher's plausible criticism to this approach is that "if the human essence is conceived non teleologically, then it is unclear how any resulting theory of the good can possibly be action guiding."(BN, p. 221) Hurka's theory seems unable to tell us what we *should* do.

In general terms, Sher holds that non-teleological properties have great difficulty in explaining how value can rise. Therefore, the only alternative path to explore lies in teleological theories that locate the human good in the achievement of essential human goals. Possible options are subjective and objective teleological theories but the former are quickly dismissed because in tracing the good to the satisfaction of desires or choices of the agent, they do not shed light on which traits, activities and the like are more or less valuable. No subjectivist theory can account for what is worth desiring or what we should choose, so in terms of critical potential these theories are very weak and unable to offer what a perfectionist theory should offer.

By contrast, Sher focuses on a teleological unifying approach able to explain value both in experiential and non-experiential states. His central argumentative move is to identify teleological with *intentional states aiming at realizing something in the world*, at altering the world by bringing about something nonexistent before. Sher explicitly affirms that "the world's failure to contain a thing of the valuable type requires that it be altered to bring a thing of that type into existence." (BN, p. 233) On this view, intentional states are the obvious candidates for sources of value, desires and choices call for adjustments in the world that conform the world to them. Of course, desires and choices may, on the one hand, be directed at impossible or unrealizable objects and, on the other, concern non-valuable or negative goals. So, a plausible criterion of selection should be identified.

Sher holds that intentional states are "firmly anchored in the natural world". (BN, p. 232) We now face the objectivist side of his proposal that should take Sher's perfectionism beyond individual desires and choices. He needs some objectivist features that make sense of and legitimize his taking distance from subjectivism. The teleological (and intentional) states designed to be factual grounds of value have to satisfy two requirements: firstly, the *depth requirement*, according to which a relevant goal has to stand in some appropriate relation to the person himself, otherwise it cannot be said to contribute to the goodness of that person's life. (BN, p. 234) Secondly, Sher proposes the *distance requirement*, according to which a goal may provide a standard of assessment of a person's life, if it stands at enough distance from him to afford a critical perspective on his life. With these requirements Sher expresses no more than two ethical instances that are current grain in the literature on the good life. On the one hand, the distance requirement expresses what other perfectionist theories translate in terms of *critical potential*: a perfectionist conception must offer each individual accessible tools for a self-revision of one's style of life. From this point of view, subjectivist theories are unable to satisfy the distance requirement, unless they make a move towards hypothetical or informed desires. On the other hand, the depth requirement expresses what is often called in the debate the 'endorsement condition'. No discussion about the agent's good life makes any sense, unless the goals in question have been internalized and belong entirely to the agent's life.

The two requirements make opposite claims that cannot be answered in one move. Thus, to move beyond subjectivism, we need to identify "goals that are independent both of all actual desires and choices and of all hypothetical ones." (BN, p. 236) Sher's solution is that near-unavoidable and near-universal goals satisfy both the depth and the distance requirement. They belong to the agent so deeply that they are presupposed by all of his specific desires and choices. The danger is that a goal an agent cannot avoid pursuing is also his in a deep sense because of a pathological compulsion he cannot resist. Furthermore, if an agent shares a goal with all others similarly situated, the distance requirement would be satisfied but we would have no tool to criticize goals sought by large groups of people (an obvious example might be that of Nazi Germany).

Sher is well aware that, on this argument, near unavoidable and near universal goals cannot provide the right combination of distance and depth. His way out of the impasse is to show that the satisfaction of each requirement depends on *both* features, near universality and near unavoidability. Firstly, the depth requirement is not satisfied by a goal being merely unavoidable because also pathological compulsions may be included. A goal, by contrast, belongs deeply enough to its possessor when it is widely shared, when it is not a fluke agents cannot avoid pursuing. Sher emphasizes that being near universal a goal does not depend on particular features or psychological make up of a certain person. Secondly, in order to overcome the weakness of near universality alone, with respect to the distance requirement (if-all members of a certain society happen to pursue a goal, we still do not know whether that goal is worth pursuing), Sher notes that when a near universal goal is also such that virtually no one can avoid pursuing it, the question of its worthiness simply does not arise. Sher goes as far as saying that there is "something about our constitution [that] makes our pursuit of it inevitable." (BN, p. 239) Goals of this kind are suitable touchstones for the evaluation of all other goals.

In conclusion, Sher's attempt to found his perfectionist theory on objectivist features keeps his position quite close to Aristotelian essentialism, as he admits. He qualifies his theory as "a kind of poor man's Aristotelianism" (BN, p. 240), an empirical substitute for a teleological essentialism. Sher insists on distinguishing his position from essentialism and its metaphysical implications but it is quite doubtful as to whether his argument is actually successful. It seems that an essentialist theory does not fare any worse in terms of critical distance than Sher's own theory. His argument against essentialism hinges on two far-fetched questions: "(1) is it better that there be humans or biologically similar organisms who lack the goals that humans necessarily pursue? and (2) if such biologically similar beings existed instead of humans, would their lives be better or worse?" (BN, p. 240) According to Sher, essential goals do not provide enough critical distance to answer those questions but, he concludes, neither should we ask them because some goals cannot be altered, they "are the inseparable components of any world in which we could conceivably take an interest." (BN, p. 241)

Sher's final discussion shows clearly what was hidden in the first presentation of his objective list: rather than just being unconnected intuitions, the items on the list rely on some kind of foundation on human nature. Rather than appealing to (metaphysical) essentialism, Sher uses the empirical argument that most people (near-universality), most of the time (near-inescapability) pursue certain goals. However, once he uses the argument that a world in which humans lacked the goal of knowing, using rational activity or achieving mutual understanding and care, would not hold any interest for us, he is appealing to the core meaning of essentialism, though not to its formal structure. The lack of the formal structure of essentialism, however, leaves the door open to charges of essentialists such as Hurka's: if a capacity for knowledge can be described as a near-universal and near-inescapable feature of human beings and as intrinsically good, what of other capacities, such as those for aggression and domination, that seem to have the same features? Should we take them as intrinsically good as well?[58]

Finally, we can conclude by returning to an issue already put forward in our introductory remarks. Sher's unconnected list of objective goods does not amount to an ideal of human flourishing able to provide coherent individual and political orientation, so it is defective both from the point of view of the good life and from that of a liberal political theory. This charge is grounded in the contrast between Sher's and similar objective list theories, on the one hand, and the classical perfectionist tradition, on the other. This was meant to offer, as in the case of Aristotle and Aquinas, an ideal of human flourishing constituted by the practice of the virtues, whereas Sher wishes to extract some of its main constituents from that ideal, such as the development of one's abilities, moral goodness and rational activity. One wonders why the state should promote these abstract and controversial concepts – which of our abilities should be developed? Should we understand moral goodness only as acting on the grounds of moral reasons? – rather than developing a comprehensive account of excellences as constituents of a *good character*. The proposal of such an account is the task of sect. 5.

TRACES OF A DIFFERENT PERFECTIONISM

If the argument in section 2 on the inadequacy of 'rights talk' to ground an alliance between liberalism and natural law theory is founded and plausible, sections 3 and 4 do not seem to bring clear progress. Both Hurka and Sher take very different leads from the original promises of perfectionist theories such as Aristotle's. Hurka's maximizing consequentialism and Sher's objective list theory appear failing with regard to the Aristotelian ideal. In my view, the basic failure is a reductive understanding of the human good. (1) Both theorists show no or little connection between their view of the human good and what I would call 'rationality in action', that is, deliberation and pondering of different means to reach a certain end and between different ends. Although both give pride of place to rationality in their theories, none of them understands rationality as infused in the ideal of the good life and spelled out in the exercise of the virtues (as in Aristotle's *eudaimonia*). Their escape from the Aristotelian 'moralistic understanding' of the human good brings about truncated views which cannot restore the integrity of human flourishing. (2) On the same line of thought they undervalue the role of emotions and desires with regard to the complex realization of human flourishing. (3) To the degree to which Hurka's and Sher's theories reject 'moralistic' contaminations, they remain open to that further evaluation that we unavoidably make on prudential views of the human good.

The ethics of virtues quickly examined in section 1 has the theoretical resources to redress these weaknesses but it needs some systematization and clarification among its plural and conflictual strands. Such an attempt has been quite successfully made and prepares the way for locating our proposal.[59] Following Nussbaum's taxonomy, I can quite safely assume that my perfectionist views are close to the work of authors such as McDowell, Wiggins, Richardson, Sherman and Nussbaum herself. [cit.] Perhaps, none of them would like to be associated with the perfectionist views I develop in what follows, but a few basic points from their theorizing apprises my perfectionist proposal, introduced as *agency goods perfectionism*.

The first priority I wish to emphasize is the crucial place of reason in directing the functioning of virtues through deliberation and, so, in *regulating* the pursuit of substantive goods. Reason also has an important role in balancing and organizing the drives arising from desires: these should not be thwarted nor should they receive limitless satisfaction because the (perfectionist) ideal that flows from the virtues aims at a *specifically* human life. From the variety of desires that human beings experience we can derive a second priority which brings together some of the above mentioned thinkers and 'agency goods perfectionism' (cf. sect 5.1): there is a plurality of qualitatively heterogeneous goods human beings normally pursue rather than just an homogeneous measure, such as utility, that can cover whatever people want. This point has the merit of focusing our attention on the complexity of Aristotelian ideals of the good life (such as agency goods perfectionism) in which the key value of *excellences* cannot be adequately rendered by a maximizing consequentialist view – nor by any list of objective goods, notwithstanding their diversity. Lastly, (although less discussed in my account of agency goods perfectionism) the third priority emerging from some of the best reflection on virtue ethics (for example, McDowell, Murdoch and Sherman) is a special attention for the place of emotion in reasoning about the good. This is an important legacy to bear in mind, while exploring my perfectionist proposal because usually perfectionist theories are so focused on objective goods or maximization the emotional side of human life is forgotten.

Agency Goods Perfectionism

What is worth emphasizing in our perfectionist proposal and connects with our introductory discussion on virtue ethics is that we wish to propose a version of perfectionism centred on an account of the virtues which amounts to a *partial* conception of human flourishing. We shall call this conception *agency goods perfectionism*. It holds that 'character', constituted by a unified set of virtues, offers a critical potential compatible with liberalism – and overlaps the core ideas of natural law theory, as we shall see. Since we explicitly derive our perfectionist conception from Aristotle's ethics, we should be careful to emphasize how agency goods perfectionism does not run any risk of incompatibility with liberalism. *Eudaimonia* has usually been taken as a full-blown ideal of 'happiness', including many objective goods the agent should pursue in his life. Such a view has been rejected by most liberals because it threatens the freedom of each individual to subjectively define what is good for him. By contrast, we shall take Aristotle's conception of *eudaimonia* and the virtues as a perfectionist proposal which does not prescribe the pursuit of substantive goods but *regulates* individual pursuits. It is regulative insofar as its *ethical* strength is constituted by *eudaimonia* and the virtues, which restrain any subjective definition of the good. It is a *perfectionist* proposal in our broad definition insofar as *eudaimonia* and the virtues represent a critical potential based on the idea of human improvement. However, improvement is only conceived in terms of the exercise of ethical excellences or excellences of character (the virtues) and does not prescribe the pursuit of any substantive ends. This perfectionism is, in a sense, based on an 'objectivist conception of the good', namely, the idea of human improvement, but it is not based on an objectivist conception of substantive goods, i.e. the ends worth pursuing by human beings.

We contend that the idea of character, as constituted by a certain set of virtues, connects virtue ethics with agency goods perfectionism. On the grounds of what has been outlined in sect. 1 we can spell out some of the main features of virtue ethics congenial to agency goods perfectionism: (1) its being agent centred, so that the concept of right action is based on that of the virtuous agent, rather than the other way round, as happens in utilitarianism and Kantian theory; (2) its being concerned with Being rather than Doing, that is, with answering the question 'what sort of agent should I be?' rather than the question 'what sort of action should I do?'; (3) its taking certain areteic concepts, such as good, excellence and virtue, as basic rather than deontic, such as right, duty and obligation.[60]

Although these features may be not subscribed by all virtue authors, they represent a plausible core of virtue ethics which may work as a bridge toward that conception of human flourishing so far neglected by virtue ethics, as noticed before. Now, our bridge has to connect at least three separated theoretical islands: not only virtue ethics and agency goods perfectionism but also natural law theory. In order to check whether this is possible we should, at this point, provide a brief outline for agency goods perfectionism and one for natural law theory (the latter is postponed to section 6). Once some parallel structures are put in place, we may have the necessary conceptual tools to advance a more detailed analysis of these three views.

The Place of Virtues in Agency Goods Perfectionism

Different perfectionist approaches have been founded on human nature (Aristotle), intuition (Raz), or a theory of organic wholes (Nozick). We believe that contemporary liberal societies can accommodate a perfectionist approach only if this is respectful of the large variety of styles of life and comprehensive conceptions of the good we face. So, no perfectionist theory can be based on a narrow and rigid account of human flourishing. We may wish to outline a *vague but still thick* account of human flourishing,[61] that is, one in which we provide a general framework of intrinsic goods to be filled in with more detailed descriptions case by case. Martha Nussbaum's hermeneutically founded account of human virtues[62] is a helpful starting point for our account of perfectionism. She argues that in basic spheres of human conduct where we cannot help choosing and acting, such as our bodily appetites, the giving and taking of money, our physical vulnerability, etc., we can give right and wrong responses. We can give a *thin* description of right responses in terms of virtues, such as temperance in the first sphere and generosity and courage respectively in the second and third spheres. To act with temperance in the sphere of bodily appetites means to act in the right way, although what temperance concretely requires in the situation is to be conceived according to the cultural context of the agent. What was the appropriate exercise of temperance in ancient Athens may not be so in contemporary Italy. Although our account of agency goods is flexible enough to allow large variations through cultural contexts, it is also perfectionist in excluding "wrong" conceptions of the good. These will be identified by "wrong" responses in the basic spheres of human experience we have just mentioned. However, most of our life choices, concerning substantive goods and careers, for example, keep their legitimate status when agency goods are exercised.

Now, we may accept a perfectionist theory but as liberals we do not wish the state to impinge on our styles of life, although we recognize that the public sphere can promote general conditions of the good life that do not pre-empt individual freedom of choice.[63] Those who reject indiscriminately any public engagement with criteria of the good life or human flourishing are doing a disservice to liberal theory insofar as they conceive the liberal state as necessarily separate and independent from the quality of life of its citizens. Very recent experiences (e.g. the current world economic crisis) clearly show that not only actions of state institutions but also world dynamics deeply affect individual lives. Politics (the organization of public institutions) and ethics (individual choices for the good life) are deeply interconnected, so the theoretical strategy of continuity seems to respond better to experience. By contrast, on the discontinuist strategy a liberal state should apply its policies without being concerned with the kind of life its citizens live.

The central idea is "the good life" or "human flourishing" which refers to the quality of a person's life as a whole. This idea may be filled in at various levels. The most general level includes, as its constituents, what we have called *agency goods*, virtues or qualities of character which work as modes of choosing in basic spheres of human conduct where we cannot help deciding. We should emphasize that our perfectionist view is a *partial* view of human flourishing or the good life. In promoting the exercise of agency goods we do not claim to suggest all that matters to an individual's way of living. This comes to consist also in a certain set of prudential goods and in other purely subjective choices. Rather, in promoting agency goods we promote what has most reasons to be shared. In this sense 'human flourishing' or 'the good life' or 'the well-lived life' are just partial concepts but with better normative foundations than more extensive ones.

Nussbaum's account can be very helpful in offering a foundation for, and identification of, agency goods. On a less general level we have *prudential goods* that contribute to someone's good life, such as aesthetic experience, human relationships, play, knowledge, etc., although they do not have to figure necessarily in every good life. Prudential goods are substantive goods, though the latter also include goods which do not directly benefit the agent (altruistic goods). What often happens is that the pursuit of one of these goods, such as knowledge, by its own nature may prevent the pursuit of other prudential goods, such as aesthetic experience or play. (At this level of theory it sounds very plausible to let in, as constituents of the good life, objective goods of the sort included within an objective list theory.) Lastly, a third category which would fill in our conception of the good life would be a *way of living* which embodies a particular ranking of agency goods and prudential goods and a particular way of realizing them.[64] In a way of living we may include not only what the agent pursues or exercises as values for their own sake - as the previous two categories - but also what he pursues instrumentally and his personal reasons for certain evaluations and rankings. My way of living, for example, can include the biographical reasons which make me a tourist entrepreneur. A way of living is not constituent of someone's good life in the same way that agency goods and prudential goods are, but it is more a particular way of organizing them, establishing priorities which are good for the person involved but not for another. Each of us has – consciously or not – a way of living because each of us pursues some goals rather than others, even though one is not always aware of what counts most in his life.

On our perfectionist view, agency goods and prudential goods, although all final, are fundamentally different. While prudential goods identify *objects of choice* we consider choice-worthy for themselves,[65] agency goods are (dispositions to engage in) *modes of choosing* in certain spheres of conduct. If we do not choose a prudential good we are still within the boundaries of the good life in opting for other prudential goods. However, if we do not exercise an agency good, such as the virtue of courage when we deal with the sphere of conduct where our bodily vulnerability is at stake, we are simply wrong.[66] Courage is what we identify as the right response, while other alternative responses, such as cowardice or rashness, are wrong.[67] We take them as inappropriate responses. Wrong responses bring our life much further from the ideal of the good life than happens when we just neglect some prudential good (whose choice is up to us, whereas agency goods are constitutive of the good life and participate in the exercise of deliberative rationality).

Given the central position of agency goods in our ideal of perfectionism, we need to add some comments on their conception here. If the opposition between agency goods and prudential goods may be taken as quite clear now, other questions may be in order with regards to agency goods. The first question to tackle is the list of our agency goods and how it is justified. Here we can refer to Nussbaum's list of basic spheres of human experience. Following Aristotle, Nussbaum lists a number of spheres of experience the most important of which are: fear of important damages, especially death; bodily appetites and their pleasures; distribution of limited resources; management of one's personal property where others are concerned; attitudes to slights and damages; association and living together; and others.[68] All these spheres define necessary circumstances of our human life and we would generally recognize a life lacking in one of these as defective, as missing something specifically human. To give a couple of examples: we could hardly recognize the life of an immortal being as a human life (literary cases of this kind strike us just because they fuel extraordinary possibilities); while social bonds, although only empirically founded, seem to constitute a part of a specifically human life. There is a general and elastic correspondence between these spheres and the list of virtues outlined by Nussbaum.[69] Courage seems in play when mortality is involved, temperance for bodily appetites and their pleasures, justice for the distribution of scarce resources, generosity in dealing with one's own property, friendliness in one's social bonds, etc. Of course, there are virtues such as magnanimity which, taken as attitudes and actions regarding one's own worth, seem culture-bound to ancient Greece, and we could think of others, such as the attitude to our natural environment, which are "progress-bound" and require naming. By and large, however, the list of basic spheres and corresponding agency goods is justified by their being accepted despite any distinction of time and place. We can still recognize what is good and bad in literary cases from the past or from very foreign cultures because their virtues and vices still correspond to our 'thin' descriptions.[70] Thin descriptions of what courage or justice are, need to be filled in according to specific circumstances of place and time, as already mentioned, but holding that the right response is courage rather than cowardice or rashness is inescapable from the human condition. When fear of severe harm to our body and even death are concerned we admire the courageous person rather than the coward or the rash one. There is no personal intuition here to identify what is virtue and what is vice but a large convergence of shared opinions through time and space.[71]

The Idea of Nature

So far we have, firstly, introduced virtue ethics and identified its main normative claims whose potentialities for liberal theory have been mainly - we have claimed - neglected in favour of another general normative discourse: rights-theory. Secondly, we have argued that rights-theory has many limitations affecting its 'performance' as a substantive normative theory with regard to perfectionist alternatives. Thirdly, we have proposed the outline of a theory named agency good perfectionism which both connects correctly with the perfectionist tradition and embodies a substantive view of human goodness that, we hold, is compatible with liberal pluralism. Keeping agency goods perfectionism in the background, we have reviewed both Hurka's maximizing perfectionism and Sher's objective list theory: neither is comparable with that point of balance among the main constituents of human nature, such as reason, desires and passions, that characterizes agency goods perfectionism.

In what follows we shall first address the idea of nature whose importance in the tradition of substantive ethics has been paramount. In time, however, its theoretical uses have been very different (from the ancient opposition between natural law and local conventions to contemporary ethical naturalism) but what remains its most precious content is the idea of 'natural reason' and its location in the agent. This is what we shall pursue in natural law theory in opposition to those contemporary versions which buy a substantive ethics at the expense of a well-balanced philosophical anthropology. Our final steps will be, firstly, an argument in favour of a virtue-based view of natural law which largely overlaps agency goods perfectionism and, secondly, a critical review of new natural law theory, whose substantive ethics, based on a list of objective goods, entirely misses the point of a well-balanced philosophical anthropology.

Natural law tradition is the ancient and venerable tradition within which all concepts we have discussed so far - such as virtue, perfection, character, natural rights and objective good - have taken shape and developed. Among NL strengths especially relevant is its being an objectivist theory to be inscribed in the same range with perfectionist and objectivist theories. Paradoxically, objectivism is criticized nowadays within the ethical debate at least as much as it was praised in ancient times, when NL was taken as a superior moral system to be appealed to against the uncertainties, deviations and mistakes of local social and legal conventions. In the work of ancient philosophers, such as Plato, Aristotle and the Stoics, insofar as they can be summoned up in the NL tradition, an objectivist ethics has the merit of offering a 'critical potential' against local conventions often weakened by false beliefs, etc. Similarly, the great construction of Roman law, summarized in the *Corpus Iuris Civilis* by Justinian, conveys the distinction between *ius civile* (the interest of one particular community), *ius gentium* (international law) and *ius naturale* (what is always good and fair). The origin of the doctrine of NL within Roman Law dates back to Cicero's appropriation of Stoicism. Cicero founds "true (natural) law on right reason, corresponding to nature, universal, constant and eternal."[72] This foundation relies uncontroversially on a common human nature which was as much a shared idea in ancient times, as it is disputed in contemporary philosophy. *Ius naturale* was presumably called on to redress eventual wrong directions in *ius civile* and *ius gentium*: so we might say that the capacity of the critical potential of NL is confirmed in Roman Law.

The ancient conception of nature is stronger and more profound than contemporary foundations on nature such as Hurka's. The idea of nature has enjoyed admiration and consideration in times of oppression or when local conventions rule because it can work as a critical standpoint against existing moral and legal rules. By contrast, in times of freedom and moral pluralism, the idea of nature is perceived as a constraint and a threat of oppression in moral matters. It seems as if 'nature' should be invoked as the necessary counterweight to individual freedom of choice. This explains why liberal political theories want to keep a wide berth from the idea of nature, perceived as a threat to individual freedom, and also why contemporary approaches to ethical naturalism, such as Hursthouse's and Foot's, just go half the distance toward the ideal of nature.[73] They wish to use a scientific approach to human nature as an objective foundation of ethics but the place of reason, for example, in Hursthouse's account is not as crucial as to prescribe the right way in which humans should live their lives. There is no right way to live, Hursthouse admits, but only a 'rational way of going on' which is 'any way we can rightly see as good'. This is surely a non controversial suggestion in the pluralistic environment of liberal democracies but it is no great progress from the point of view of value orientation.

For a safe way to define natural law we can find a solid answer in the most well-known name in its tradition, Thomas Aquinas:

'natural law is the light of natural reason whereby we discern what is good and what is evil.' It can guide our reason insofar as it is the light of the Divine reason.[74] Following this definition, Rhonheimer emphasizes, "a Thomistic theory of natural law must [...] be a theory of moral knowledge and of its principles.[...] Natural reason has a truth-attaining, illuminating power: it is a 'light' intrinsic to our soul, an expression of the fact that human persons are created in the image of God."[75] It seems to me that these lines direct our attention primarily to the theological grounding of NL but also, importantly, to what is emphasized by the twelfth century canonist Huguccio: "the natural law is said to be a judgment of reason, namely a motion proceeding from reason, directly or indirectly."[76] So, it seems to me that Jean Porter correctly distinguishes not only specific moral norms in NL but also a fundamental capacity for moral judgment.[77] We are, thus, back to a crucial feature of the ethics of virtues mentioned at the beginning (cf. sect. 1), as what marks the difference between classical NL and modern NL authors such as Grotius, on the one hand, while, on the other, a capacity for moral judgments is an aspect of the ideal of agency goods perfectionism I have advocated above.

We should now introduce another contemporary version of natural law theory, usually called 'new natural law theory' (NNL), which differs from the classical version under several accounts. What is relevant for us now is the NNL rejection of the normativity of 'nature', charged with being too reductive of ethics. While writers in ethical naturalism do not accept the limitations nature imposes on modern freedom of choice, NNL authors connect the appeal to nature with an appeal to metaphysics which is, they believe, unacceptable for contemporary agents. They aim to substitute nature with 'objectivity'. Finnis in the *Fundamentals of Ethics* stresses what he defines the 'radical practicality of ethics' that should not be subject to the reductivist strategy.[78] By 'reductivism' Finnis means the theoretical explication of moral concepts in terms of a metaphysical, cognitive foundation. A moral theory is 'reduced' or 'falls back' on a metaphysical basis in order to have normative validity. Finnis's move is disruptive of a central thesis in natural law according to which human nature or human essence plays a crucial role in determining the human good and the concrete goods to be sought. In Aristotelian terms, human goods or ends (the final causes) are connected to, and depend on, the human function (formal cause) or essence. By contrast, Finnis wishes to eliminate relativism and subjectivism in ethics by relying on the concept of 'objectivity' rather than that of 'nature'.[79] He suggests that his list of basic goods is objective because they are self-evident or *per se nota* propositions and are not reducible to facts about human nature.

Before continuing to consider the substantive ethical views deriving from classical NL and NNL, we should recall that Thomistic ethics depends entirely on an account of human nature, its capacities and its final cause: happiness as *beatitudo*. In turn, this account develops as a philosophical anthropology, focusing on the functioning of desires, passions, will and intellect, insofar as they are related to the virtues.[80] Whatever else ca be said about NL and perfectionism, this much should be kept in mind as we proceed.

VIRTUES IN NATURAL LAW THEORY

In order to reach some kind of tentative positive conclusion in our assessment of the three most important contemporary contenders in the field of the human good, it is now time to inquire into the substantive ethical views of NL theory. The plural is required, of course, by the (conflictual) coexistence of classical NL, based on the virtues, and of NNL, based on fundamental goods. If the assumptions put forward in section 1 are plausible, the alliance of natural law theory with a perfectionist liberalism through virtue ethics should now be confirmed, although the NNL alternative proposal deserves critical assessment. Thus, our crucial steps are now, firstly, to inquire into the virtues of the NL tradition and verify their similarity (and overlapping) with the virtues discussed in contemporary virtue ethics. Secondly, we shall outline NNL ethical views and assess its position on the virtues, relying both on theories offered to present debate by some of its most influential members, such as Grisez and Finnis, and on Finnis's account of Aquinas's views on practical reason.

In commenting on the virtues of the NL tradition there is an initial basic caution to note: this tradition is notoriously split into two equally important halves represented by Christian and secular virtues. While the latter are theorized first in Greek ethical thought (by way of example consider the cardinal virtues of practical wisdom, justice, courage and temperance), the former can be taken in two ways: firstly, as special (theological) virtues that only Christians have and care about because of their conception of God (such as faith, hope and charity); secondly, as 'infused' virtues that God implants in us (not only our theological but also cardinal virtues depend on God's infusion, according to this view). It is quite obvious that theological virtues are specific to Christian believers and there is no claim of an overlapping with contemporary secular views on the virtues. Rather, what deserves our analysis is the real status of 'infused' virtues in the work of the foremost defender of Christian ethics: Thomas Aquinas.

Under the label 'infused' virtues the Scholastics included all those virtues, as the cardinal ones, belonging to the secular tradition, but with an important difference: infused virtues are received from God 'to some degree'. The working out of the degree of reception vs. acquisition through effort of the moral virtues is our task now. We should discern different Scholastic views, moving between two poles: the Augustinian position, that virtue is a gift of grace and the Aristotelian position, that virtue is an achievement of human effort. What is at stake is more than a doctrinal disagreement: our attempt at describing a parallel between natural law theory and liberal perfectionism can be successful only if we can identify an understanding of the virtues in natural law which leaves room for human effort.

If we follow the careful reconstruction by John Inglis,[81] a useful starting point is the suggestion that Aquinas constructed the second part of his *Summa Theologiae* on the grounds of William Peraldus's *Summa de Vitiis et Virtutibus* (around 1250). Moving from within an Augustinian background of ideas, Peraldus did not wish to reduce human beings to puppets caused to act by divine grace. His way out of the Augustinian problem of human freedom was to distinguish between infused virtues God produces in us 'without us' and the cardinal virtues for which human effort is required. However, human effort is required only to prepare oneself to receive the cardinal virtues from God. Peraldus goes beyond Augustine in allowing human effort a role but does not go as far as admitting that human beings can cooperate with God in the acquisition of the moral virtues.[82] It was, then, up to Aquinas to reconsider and reduce still further the Augustinian authority on the issue of virtues.

Aquinas, faithful to his great guide, Aristotle, wished to confer a greater role to human beings in the acquisition of the virtues. This works through habitual human activity producing moral virtues in cooperation with God, since activities conforming with nature and received from God, appear as cooperation with God.[83] Thus, while at the higher level the theological virtues perfect people in relation to the highest good of *beatitudo,* people need to be perfected also in relation to those physical objects and other people which are the causes of their actions. The infused moral virtues come into shape and direct lower appetites to their ultimate end, as happens with the infused virtues of temperance and courage; whereas - and this is the crucial point for us - the acquired virtues of temperance and courage direct a person's action with regard to his highest good in the worldly life, but there is a strict relationship between the two forms of virtue. Rather than being of no help, as Augustine thought, the acquired virtue prepares the person to receive its infused counterpart. This does not happen through a radical replacement that makes the acquired virtue disappear, because Aquinas conceives the relation in terms of a harmonious transition in which the infused virtue builds upon the acquired one and strengthens its operation.[84]

This view of Christian virtues is clearly the most compatible with our liberal perfectionism based on the virtues because it leaves room for the worldly highest good, although locating the divine good at a superior level. However, most important to our purposes is that Aquinas's reconstruction grants compatibility and cooperation between acquired and infused moral virtues. For example, while acquired temperance serves bodily health and the general balance of one's good - civil - life, infused temperance can supervene and transform the final cause, directing the work of the acquired virtue to the highest good of *beatitudo.* So, rather than finding an opposition between two incompatible ethical conceptions, we find that "acquired virtue can enable one to move more easily toward the final end."[85] Such a general scheme of compatibility can make room for, and offer keys to interpretation, as in the case of temperance and abstention. Once we accept the idea of a continuum between acquired and infused virtues, that is between the worldly and the non-worldly final cause, the point of balance to identify in each case, according to its specific circumstances, has to be drawn also in light of physical desires and their satisfaction. If infused virtues build on acquired ones, the account of these starts from those spheres of physical needs and desires that inextricably belong to human nature - then, there is continuity rather than opposition between happiness from the acquired virtues in this world and *beatitudo* from infused virtues at the divine level.[86]

New Natural Law Fundamental Goods

It is now time to challenge the competing view within natural law theory which threatens to undermine our project of a common ground between secular and religious ethics, passing through a conception of virtues. By contrast, new natural law theory holds that a substantive ethics has to consist in a list of objective basic goods which are - famously - self-evident, intrinsic and open to pursuit by a limitless number of people in a limitless number of ways. An initial example of these goods is provided by Finnis's list in *Natural Law and Natural Rights* which enumerates: knowledge, life, play, aesthetic experience, sociability (friendship), practical reasonableness and religion.[87] A far more developed and sophisticated list is offered by May who, summarizing the views of NNL, distinguishes five reflexive or existential goods in which choice enters for their very definition and which have 'harmony' as a common theme, including marriage, harmony between and among individuals and groups of persons, harmony among one's feelings, judgments and actions or peace of conscience and harmony with God or religion. Furthermore, we have three substantive goods which do not require choice for their definition: life (including health, bodily integrity and the transmission of life), knowledge of the truth and appreciation of beauty, lastly excellence in work and play.[88]

Whatever our reception of these lists of basic goods or principles, it should be emphasized that these are principles of practical reason, not moral principles. The morality aspect of NNL comes in with the 'basic requirements of practical reasonableness': these are defined as modes of responsibility and specify ways of choosing not incompatible with a will oriented toward *integral human fulfilment* – NNL neologism for the idea of the highest good. [cit.]

Given the general slant of this paper, two short remarks are to the point here. Firstly, as to content, basic goods only seem to represent a set of *prudential* goods, selected from a large and varied set which has been increasing over time. A list of basic goods is weak both because the foundation of just those items rather than others is intuition[89] (as in all lists of objective goods) and because often the pursuit of some prudential goods may prevent the pursuit of others (cf. sect. 5). Secondly, as to structure, a list of basic goods – although referred to a highest good such as 'integral human fulfilment' – cannot amount to a comprehensive ideal of the good life, able to cover all basic spheres of human experience. It is lacking in terms of that well-balanced view of human flourishing that interweaves the basic components of human anthropology, such as reason, desires and passions. This view has been exemplified in agency goods perfectionism.

An important task in our assessment of NNL is, at this point, to give due consideration to their views about the virtues. It is, therefore, crucial to our proper understanding of NNL ethical views to check how its authors regard the issue of virtues in classical natural law. Correctly, Finnis focuses on the structure of deliberation and choice in order to identify what is central in Aquinas's ethical discussion. The first crucial postulate in Finnis's position is that in Aquinas's doctrine there is a number of basic human goods not fully reducible to any one more fundamental good and that these provide the first principles of practical reason. NNL advocates hold that these basic goods are incommensurable, although all are unified by their relationship to the absolutely first principle in Thomistic ethics that 'good is to be done and pursued and bad avoided'. Much of Finnis's argument seems to revolve around two points developed in note 92 of his *Aquinas*.[90] Firstly, the ends of human life (principles of practical reasonableness) are more basic than all the virtues, being pre-existent in our practical reason as 'naturally known principles', prior to (and making possible) the development of any virtue.[91]

In referring explicitly Aquinas's thought on the virtues, Finnis states that the good of virtue is the *bonum rationis*, "both an intelligible good in which a reasonable person is interested and the good of that person's being interested in it and sufficiently well-integrated (mind integrated with will and each with sub-rational desires and powers) to choose it and to put it into practice."[92] We are also told that excellence and strength of character involve a disposition to act with *intelligent* love in pursuit of basic human goods.[93] So, although this account makes room for the virtues, it is basically for *the virtue* of practical reasonableness or prudence, as we have already noticed, not for the single moral virtues as spheres of balance between specific sets of desires and reason. Furthermore, and most importantly, in Finnis's interpretation of Aquinas the virtues still have a merely auxiliary role with regard to basic human goods which remain the crucial normative item in NNL's ethics. The good of virtue, in the sense of *bonum rationis*, commits to choose with a will toward all the basic goods of human existence, with a will toward *integral human fulfilment*, a concept which, as we already noticed, in the later work of the NNL school has substituted the traditional *beatitudo* or *felicitas*.

The second point that Finnis develops in note 92 is the view that when Aquinas refers to the human ends (basic human goods) with a singular noun (*finis*), this is often mistranslated as 'the end'. Finnis appeals to I-II q. 58 a.3 ad.2 as one of the texts which show directly that by *finis* Aquinas often means ends in the plural. The tripartition of natural inclinations to which Aquinas refers in his account makes plausible room for a plurality of basic goods such as *life, marriage, knowledge, practical reasonableness*[94], but also as specifications, *friendship, justice and harmony with God.* Lastly, Finnis concludes his list with *beatitudo* or *felicitas*, happiness in the sense of fulfilment, that is not so much an item added to the list as a synthesis of all basic human goods.[95] Finnis's translation of *beatitudo* in terms of integral human fulfilment emphasizes its being a *bonum integrum*, "presumably to signify that the perfection is a good made up of many goods."[96] If, as in the case of Aristotle, those goods stand to the integral good as parts stand to the whole, it is difficult to believe that Aquinas thinks of *beatitudo* only in terms of achievement of basic goods such as life, marriage and so on. Given their non-homogeneity, it sounds odd that they can make up a *bonum integrum*. Rather, it seems much more plausible to take *virtue in action* as the central definition of human fulfilment insofar as it is "the perfection of the human capacities involved in action."[97]

It is important to emphasize that in referring the thought of the great master of natural law, Finnis has to admit and do justice to the traditional ethical conception of the virtues, taking distance from his previous marginalization of the virtues in NLNR, where he concentrated all of his account on a list of 'basic values', while describing virtues such as courage, generosity, moderation, gentleness and the like as 'aspects of human self-determination and self-realization'. More precisely, they were taken not as basic values but as ways or modes of pursuing basic values.[98]

However, the position of NNL authors with regard to virtues is more articulated than appears from Finnis's account. Critics within contemporary natural law discourse notice that NNL authors "do not continue the Thomistic tradition regarding the cardinal virtues of prudence, justice, fortitude and temperance and the way in which Aquinas related these virtues to specific powers of the human person."[99] However, we should look at the work of the founder of NNL, Germain Grisez, to grasp the nuances of a theoretical position which understands the centrality of virtues in the moral and Christian tradition only reductively: "Much of what Scriptures and Christian teaching say on morality is expressed in the language of the virtues." [100] Although acknowledging this much, Grisez reshapes the virtues in terms of 'modes of responsibility' which stem from the 'first principle of morality': "in voluntarily acting for human goods and avoiding what is opposed to them, one ought to choose and otherwise will, those and only those possibilities whose willing is compatible with a will toward integral human fulfilment." [101]

With regard to the latter concepts we know to be crucial to NNL, virtues are associated to modes of responsibility because they do not concern specific kinds of acts. Virtues come as aspects of a personality well-integrated in itself with a morally good self. According to Grisez, such a personality is shaped by choices that go along with the first principle of morality and with modes of responsibility: the virtues embody the latter. Thereafter, a character expresses and embodies these modes.[102] In order to make the moral import of the virtues completely clear, we should verify which modes of responsibility we have. *Christian Moral Principles* expand, for example, on the following modes – that resemble deontological norms more than virtues: (1) one should not be deterred by felt inertia from acting for intelligible goods; (2) one should not be pressed by enthusiasm or impatience to act individualistically for intelligible goods; (3) one should not choose to satisfy an emotional desire except as part of one's pursuit and/or attainment of an intelligible good other than the satisfaction of the desire itself.[103] We cannot doubt that these modes and others described by Grisez derive from the core of Christian teaching, but we remain very doubtful of his view that the virtues, as dispositions of character which keep reason on balance with desires and emotions (as classical tradition teaches), can be reduced to norms prescribing certain actions and prohibiting others. Although acknowledging (without quoting him) Thomas proposed a moral theology, founded on an ethics of virtues, Grisez emphasizes that "virtues do not provide a normative source distinct from propositional principles such as the modes and the completely specific norms they generate."[104] Lastly, Grisez's reductivist position on the virtues is confirmed by his thesis that character is largely (though not entirely) the main structure of one's choices, the self which expresses and shows itself in further particular acts. So-called ethics of character (or of virtues), emphasizing character rather than particular acts, realizes a false dichotomy.[105]

The reasons behind this reductivist position on the virtues held by NNL are surely so strong to determine a sharp fracture in what Robert George calls, after Berlin, 'the central tradition of Western thought'.[106] While the central tradition, from Aristotle to Thomas, is centered on the virtues as a crucial ethical component in strengthening the moral fabric of people and society, liberalism, by contrast, introducing and emphasizing a pluralism of values, generates disgregating effects on the traditional conception of the good that George takes as hierarchical, elitist and antipluralist. In turn, a conception of the kind offered by NNL – based on the recognition of a multiplicity of fundamental human goods that can be pursued and organized in multiple ways by different persons and communities, is much more congenial to the liberal pluralism of values. The virtues of tradition are identified and criticized as a monolithic model of the good life conflicting with the variety of human goods, whereas the conception of fundamental human goods is taken to emphasize the diversity of ways of life available to modern citizens.[107] However, in light of the interpretation of the virtues argued for in previous sections, it is quite doubtful that the tradition of virtues can be charged with antipluralism, while NNL fundamental goods express a variety more congenial to liberal pluralism.

CONCLUSIONS

My entire discussion on substantive theories of the good so far may be misplaced or useless, if citizens in liberal societies accept some relativistic view of value, trusting at best a conception of human rights and disdaining any attempt at defining what is objectively good. However, if many signs, perceived in different quarters, have been correctly interpreted, we may plausibly identify a well-spread need for value orientation which runs on different levels in liberal societies. The revival of virtue ethics, a return of natural law theories and some perfectionist hints in liberal theory, all show a demand for a stronger connection of ethics to human needs and desires compared to what rights theories can express.

From that point of view, many versions of EV align more with their so-called universalist opponents, Kantianism and utilitarianism, rather than with NL theory and perfectionism. The threshold is given by the conception of the good embodied by these theories: relativistic theories come quite close to Kantian and utilitarian subjectivistic conceptions of the good. In turn, insofar as Kant and utilitarian masters such as Bentham and Sidgwick hold theories of virtues, they seem not to oppose EV, although still remaining on the subjectivistic side of the threshold.[108] (In truth, Kant deserves a separate discourse since his analysis of the virtues in the *Metaphysics of Morals* led a few theorists to align him with perfectionist theory).

I have tried to argue that EV becomes a more interesting contender in the ethical and political arena, if taken at its best, that is, as conveying a substantive (objectivist) conception of the good in terms of human excellences. Reviving a vocabulary and a framework of thinking in terms of human excellences (virtues) brings back to the fore human nature with desires, needs, character, etc. The general idea put forward from the beginning of this paper, is that EV conveys a conception of the good deserving a more careful treatment than EV theorists would care to concede. We have attempted to show that agency goods perfectionism makes a good job in proposing a substantive ethics connected with a philosophical anthropology in which reason, desires and passions realize an ideal balance.

Starting from a liberal political framework, we have tried to argue, on the one hand, that individual ethics (e.g. how an agent pursues his good life or wellbeing) and politics cannot be detached from one another because a state has to worry about the style of life of its citizens. Contemporary contenders in the moral and political fields, such as rights theories, cannot go all the way in connecting ethics and politics. Following well-established lines of argument, such as those of Raz and Finnis, we have argued that 'rights talk' stops short of including important ethical concepts, such as individual flourishing, the common good or solidarity. On the other hand, we have argued that, once the general demand for value-orientation is found plausible, and different substantive normative theories assessed, the view that starts from EV and runs through agency goods perfectionism and classical natural law theory seems to express a well-balanced ideal of human flourishing in which the main components of any philosophical anthropology, such as reason, desires and passions have their due. By contrast, we have generally argued that contemporary contenders in the field of substantive normative theories such as objective list theories and NNL, do not express a similar balanced ideal.

I have tried to argue that there is a common core of ideas that runs through the three schools of theories most concerned with the theory of the good. It is a core conception that can be outlined in terms of virtues with small substantial differences between the secular (liberal) and the Christian (natural law) field. The most relevant points in this conception can be summarized in the following way: (1) the acquisition and exercise of the virtues resembles that of practical skills: both become hard-wired in a person's constitution and will be exercised in accordance with character (no need of explicit thought to virtuous acts, given certain situations);[109] (2) the functioning of the virtues is a matter of rational deliberation rather than feelings and it is the element of reason that deserves objective relevance and evaluation; (3) lastly, assessing goodness in terms of virtues points out a reading of 'what it is like to be a good person' that may be helpful to answer questions about value orientation.

This short outline summarizes some of the basic views we have expressed in *agency goods perfectionism*. In turn, agency goods perfectionism presents a view of the human good that can be endorsed by classical NL (without explicit conflict with Christian virtues), while eliminating a group of other contenders for different reasons: (a) perfectionists such as Hurka (see above, sect. 3) or virtue theorists such as Hursthouse and Foot (see above, sect. 6) place a great weight in their theories on (human) nature but, in times of ethical relativism, they do not wish to embody evaluative considerations that would 'moralise' their views (and avoid implausible consequences); (b) objective list theories try to answer a demand for some degree of objectivism in our conceptions of well-being but end up proposing lists based on intuition, whose included goods are no more plausible than some excluded ones, but surely do not amount to an acceptable conception of how to live well; (c) lastly, NNL theories show some of the same weaknesses of OLT, worsened by the fact that they include more controversial goods, such as 'religion', without distinguishing the possibility of *imperfecta* from *perfecta beatitude*. Quite likely, retrieving some of Aquinas's wisdom expressed in the central position of the virtues in his ethics, would improve the plausibility of these theories.

In conclusion, we should note that the plausibility of the argument for the overlapping between agency goods perfectionism and natural law theory in the area of virtues (if not entirely persuasive) at least shows that the traditional theory of the good from which liberalism developed deserves more careful consideration. Real life choices and activities revolve around experiences of the good, wellbeing and flourishing at least as much as, or more than, experiences of right and justice. Thus, it is surely plausible to assume that further steps in the argument, following this attempt, will only improve the moral and political self-understanding of the liberal society.

Notes

1. E. Anscombe, "Modern Moral Philosophy" in *Philosophy*, 133, 1958.
2. Since A. MacIntyre, *After Virtue*, Notre Dame University Press, Notre Dame, 1981.
3. Cf. I. Murdoch, *The Sovereignty of the Good*, Schocken Books, 1971; S.Wolf, "Moral Saints" in *Journal of Philosophy*, 79, 1982; L. Blum, "Moral Exemplars. Reflections on Schindler, the Trocmes and Others" in *Midwest Studies in Philosophy* Vol. XIII, University of Notre Dame Press, Notre Dame, 1988.

4. Cf. R. Louden, "On Some Vices of Virtue Ethics" in R. Kruschwitz and R. Roberts (eds.), *The Virtues*, Wadsworth, Belmont (Ca.), 1987.

5. Cf. Ph. Foot, *Virtues and Vices*, University of California Press, Berkeley, 1978.

6. J. Driver, "The Virtues and Human Nature" in R. Crisp (ed.), *How Should One Live?*, Clarendon Press, Oxford, 1996, p. 113.

7. *Ibid.*

8. Cf. M. Stocker, "How Emotions Reveal Value", in *How Should One Live?*, *cit.*, pp. 173-90.

9. A. MacIntyre, *After Virtue*, Notre Dame University Press, Notre Dame, 1984.

10. Cf. A. Rorty, "Virtues and Their Vicissitudes" in *Midwest Studies*, *cit.*, pp. 136-8.

11. I doubt that this characterization applies to Kant as it applies to Kantian theories because Kant's ethical thought is more complex and less deontological that what orthodox interpretation supposes. Cf. A.Wood, *Kant's Ethical Thought*, Cambridge University Press, Cambridge, 1999.

12. The first four points of our outline are quite shared by a large number of authors in the ethics of virtues but by no means can they all be taken to describe the core of the ethics of virtues. On the one hand, the usual opposition between ethics of virtues and the Kantian and utilitarian theories is misleading because also the latter dwell largely on the concepts of virtues and character, as so well argued by M.Nussbaum in "Virtue Ethics : A Misleading Category", *Journal of Ethics*, 3, 1999. On the other hand, Nussbaum herself identifies a narrow common ground among defenders of virtue ethics, including concern with the agent, his choice and action; with the character of the inner moral life and settled patterns of motive, emotion and reasoning; within the overall course of the agent's moral life. Cf. ibid., p 170. Such a core conception is not foreign to founders of moral philosophy such as Kant, Bentham or Sidgwick, although it was foreign to Kantians and utilitarians doing philosophy in the '50s through to the '70s.

13. Cf. J.B. Schneewind, "The Misfortunes of Virtue" in *Ethics* 101, 1990. It should be underlined that one of the main aims of this paper lies in the attempt to reinvigorate the classical view of natural law theory which, in contrast with Grotius' 'legalistic' natural law, emphasized the place of the virtues. See infra, sect. 6.

14. A remarkable exception is M. Nussbaum, "Non-Relative Virtues" in *Midwest Studies*, *cit.*, pp. 32-53.

15. Cf. Nussbaum, "Virtue Ethics: A Misleading Category", *cit.*, p. 180 ff.

16. Cf. R. Dworkin, "Foundations of Liberal Equality" in *The Tanner Lectures on Human Values*, University of Utah Press, Salt Lake City, 1991.

17. This issue cannot be the subject of this paper because it would lead us astray but it should be emphasized that 'the return of religion in the secular age' has been widely discussed in recent times. Cf. J. Habermas, *Between Naturalism and Religion: Philosophical Essays*, Polity Press, Cambridge, 2008; Ch.Taylor, *A Secular Age*, Bellknap Press, 2007.

18. Cf. J. Finnis, *Natural Law and Natural Rights*, Clarendon Press, Oxford, 1980, pp. 205-10.

19. Cf. J. Porter, *Nature as Reason*, Eerdmans, Grand Rapids (Mich.), 2005, pp 348-50; she relies on the work of B.Tierney, *Idea of Natural Rights*, Scholars Press, Atlanta, 1997, pp. 54-65.

20. This is a failure in the application of rights deeply rooted in the incompatibility of certain religious doctrines with the ethics of equal human dignity which founds human rights. In this very controversial area (where religious questions are involved) an attempt at a deeper intercultural agreement may perhaps come from the shared understanding of human development and excellence as an objective worthy of a wide-spread consent, notwithstanding religious differences.

21. Cf. Porter, *cit.*, pp. 360-1.

22. Cf. Dagger, *Civic Virtues*, Oxford University Press, Oxford, 1997, pp. 3-4. (The definitions are mine.)

23. Cf. Raz, *cit.*, pp. 196-7.

24. Cf. Finnis, *cit.*, pp. 211-6.

25. *Ibid.*, p. 214.

26. *Pace* the supporters of the Will Theory of rights who reject any grounding of rights in wellbeing or interests.

27. Cf. T. Hurka, *Perfectionism*, Oxford University Press, Oxford, 1993, p. 3.

28. Nozick's inclusion in the perfectionist field can sound puzzling for any reader familiar with *Anarchy, State and Utopia*, Basic Books, New York, 1974. But Nozick has been arguing in detail for a view of intrinsic goodness based on a conception of 'organic unity' in *Philosophical Explanations*, Clarendon Press, Oxford, 1981. It is also worth noticing that there is no explicit attempt at reviewing his previous political theory: his new considerations are only concerned with individual ethics.

29. See G.H. Von Wright, *The Varieties of the Goodness*, Routledge, New York, 1960, chap. 5.

30. Cf. T. Hurka, *cit.*, p. 3. Hurka also considers broader definitions of perfectionism, such as Hamilton's 'the full and harmonious development of all our faculties' or Rawls's 'achievement of human excellences'. Ibid., p 4.

31. It is worth noticing that usually, when people propose or discuss perfectionist theories, they refer to some version of the broad definition. This absorbs a common understanding of perfectionism, such as improving artistic or physical excellences. However, I hold that these senses are 'derived' from the original, Aristotelian, idea of 'ethical' excellences' that we try to retrieve in the 'narrow definition' (cf. below). Ethical excellences identify what most deserves to be promoted in the human being.

32. This is Sher's solution, cf. *Beyond Neutrality*, Cambridge University Press, Cambridge, 1997, pp 8-9 and Hurka, *cit.*, p. 5.

33. Hurka, *cit.*, p. 9.

34. Ivi.

35. Cf. *Ibid.*, p. 19.

36. Cf. *Ibid.*, pp. 10-14.

37. Cf. *Ibid.*, p. 17 and criticism by M. Stocker, "Some Comments on Perfectionism", in *Ethics*, 105, (Jan.) 1995, p. 388.

38. Cf. Hurka, *cit.*, p. 20.

39. This comes from Hurka's view of perfection as rationality plus the incentive to maximization.

40. *Ibid.*, p. 120.

41. Stocker, *cit.*, p. 396.

42. Hurka, *cit.*, p. 99.

43. *Ibid.*, p. 55 ff.

44. Although the political and social conditions which further the development of *eudaimonia* and the virtues can be produced by the state, this is true only at the level of political morality. At the level of individual morality, by contrast, the exercise of virtues is no question of 'production'.

45. *Ibid.*, pp. 55-6. Aristotle's quotation, however, seems to be quite misappropriate: at 1177 b 35 he says that we ought to go to all lengths to live a life that expresses our supreme element, namely the activity of contemplation or theoretical knowledge. A life expressing

understanding or contemplation is the most choice-worthy and god-like. Equating these views with maximization of some value sounds rather strange.

46. According to the Aristotelian ideal, one is or is not excellent: it is not a matter of degree, like being more or less courageous in front of the enemy. If one is courageous, he responds to the situation of danger, doing what is appropriate: he cannot maximize on courage without running the risk of excess (cf. the well-known Aristotelian vice of recklessness); similarly with generosity, temperance and the other virtues. They are not capacities, such as a talent for running fast or playing soccer that are present in degrees in people and most of us prefer to have more rather than less. Neither can we take the virtues simply as results of moral action because a virtue is, first of all, a mode of choosing (and a certain inner predisposition).

47. Michael Stocker has been particularly eloquent in commenting on the special features of friendship which do not lend themselves to maximization. Hurka's conception of 'broad perfectionism' refers to "some development of capacities or some achievement of excellence". *Perfectionism*, cit., p 4. Following Stocker, we can contest that friendship (as many other values) is neither a capacity to be developed, the greater the better, nor does it represent an achievement of excellence, similar to artistic or scientific excellence (as in Rawls's understanding of perfectionism), because friendship has to be lived through day by day, with all its good and bad aspects. Cf. M. Stocker, *Plural and Conflicting Values*, Oxford University Press, Oxford, 1990, chap. 10.

48. At the level of the Aristotelian ideal, character-friendship is perfectly good as a binary property: its goodness is or is not present. However, at the level of our everyday experience of life, we all reflect on what (a good) friendship requires in the variety of situations that each of us faces. In this case the goodness of friendship is a scalar property that can be improved or worsened, according to our responses that always strive for the better.

49. See J. Raz, *The Morality of Freedom*, Oxford University Press, Oxford, 1986; W.Galston, *Liberal Purposes*, Cambridge University Press, Cambridge, 1991.

50. See D.Parfit, *Reasons and Persons*, Oxford University Press, Oxford, 1986, Appendix I, "What Makes Someone's Life Go Best".

51. *Ibid.*, p. 493.

52. *Ibid.*, p. 499.

53. T. Scanlon, *What We Owe to Each Other*, Bellknap Press, Cambridge (Mass.), 1997.

54. Parfit agrees entirely with Aristotle about pleasure because he does not endorse his objective list just as it is but only adding that one's life goes well, if he has those good things and strongly wants them, finding pleasure in them. Cf. Parfit, *cit.*, p. 502.

55. G. Sher, *Beyond Neutrality*, Cambridge University Press, Cambridge, 1997. From now on BN.

56. Th. Hurka, *Review of 'Beyond Neutrality'*, in "Ethics" 109 (1), 1988, p. 187.

57. For example, see J.Griffin, *Wellbeing*, Oxford University Press, Oxford, 1986, chap. 4.

58. Cf. Hurka, Review, *cit.*, p. 190.

59. See M. Nussbaum, "Virtue Ethics: A Misleading Category" in *The Journal of Ethics*, 3, 1999.

60. This account is provided is provided but not subscribed by R. Hursthouse, *On Virtue Ethics*, Oxford University Press, Oxford, 1999, p. 25.

61. The expression 'thick vague conception of the good', as already noticed, is Martha Nussbaum's in "Aristotelian Social Democracy" in Richardson, Mara, Douglass (eds.), *Liberalism and the Good*, London, Kegan, 1990, p. 205.

62. M. Nussbaum, "Non-Relative Virtues", *cit.*, pp. 32-53.

63. This is not to say that all supporters of freedom will be satisfied with our arrangement. However, once freedom is considered in the context of a human life, it should be clear that its importance depends on the activities that people can realize with it. Freedom of choice allows people to realize their goals to a degree depending on eventual hindrances and so it is scalar but it is also scalar with regard to its goods. Once we accept the purposefulness of freedom of choice, the perfectionist discourse on self-restraint on the grounds of agency goods sounds more plausible. Cf. Ch. Taylor, "What's Wrong With Negative Liberty?" in *Philosophical Papers* 2, Cambridge University Press, Cambridge, 1985.

64. I have borrowed the distinction between particular categories of goods and a way of living from Joseph Chan, "Legitimacy, Unanimity and Perfectionism", in *Philosophy and Public Affairs*, 29, 2000, p. 11.

65. It is not for the individual agent to determine something to be choice-worthy in itself: choice-worthiness is already there to be picked up, although it is neither abstract – as it would be according to criteria such as Nozick's organic unity – nor absolute. Choice-worthiness, then, is beyond subjectivist choice but relies on what is good for a

specifically human life and can be detected through a hermeneutical approach *a là* Nussbaum. What is choice-worthy is usually confirmed in different societies through time and space, so it is "for us" as much as it is for our fellows similarly situated.

66. Wrongness here does not depend on 'producing bad consequences' for the agent but on refusing the correct kind of conduct from the point of view of what constitutes the good life or flourishing). Given the complexity of this ideal, what appears good (or bad) to the agent (e.g., here, now and individually) will differ from general criteria of right and wrong conduct.

67. Our definition of courage with regard to bodily vulnerability will seem a restriction of use to all those - ancients as much as contemporaries - who extend the use of courage to conduct to take in the face of evils such as bad reputation, poverty, sickness and others. We want to follow Aristotle who explicitly defines these as uses by *similarity*, while the central case of courage is that concerned with fear for the vulnerability of one's body (especially death). Cf. NE 1115a10-24.

68. Nussbaum, "Non-relative Virtues", p. 35.

69. *Ibid.*, pp. 35-6.

70. If agency goods are nothing else than virtues, why use the first term at all? Why not remain within the traditional bounds? The basic reason for my adopting 'agency goods' is that the extensive debate on the virtues as a moral theory alternative to utilitarianism or Kantianism has overloaded the term. We are taking agency goods here as a coherent set of 'internal goods' which orientate the agent's choice on all basic matters of his conduct in life. By contrast, the virtues are taken more narrowly in the contemporary debate as a form of morality, i.e. correct behaviour toward others, excluding important areas of conduct such as friendliness or our sense of humour.

71. It is worth-mentioning here that the idea of virtue has a higher degree of universality than the competing conception of 'fundamental rights' which is so often heralded now.

72. *De Republica* III.XXII, 33.

73. R. Hursthouse, *On Virtue Ethics*, Oxford University Press, Oxford, 1999; P.Foot, *Natural Goodness*, Oxford University Press, Oxford, 2001.

74. Cf. S.T. I-II, 19.4

75. M. Rhonheimer, "Review of 'Nature as Reason: A Thomistic Theory of Natural Law'", *Studies in Christian Ethics*, 19.3, 2006, pp. 362-3.

76. Lottin, pp. 109-110.

77. Cf. Porter, *cit.*, p. 14.
78. J. Finnis, *Fundamentals of Ethics*, Clarendon Press, Oxford, 1983.
79. Cf. Finnis, *cit.*, p. 10.
80. Cf. R. Pasnau, *Thomas Aquinas on Human Nature*, Cambridge University Press, Cambridge, 2002, pp. 16-22.
81. J. Inglis, "Aquinas's Replication of the Acquired Moral Virtues", *Journal of Religious Ethics*, Vol. 27, 11, 1999.
82. *Ibid.*, p. 9.
83. *Ibid.*, p. 11.
84. Cf. S.T. I-II 51.4 ad 3 and Inglis's comment, *cit.*, pp. 14-20.
85. Inglis, *cit.*, p. 22.
86. After presenting agency goods perfectionism, the account of essential spheres of human experience is by now familiar. One could even go as far as assuming that the *thin* description or right responses in terms of virtues keeps agency goods perfectionism closer to Aquinas's virtues than other perfectionist accounts.
87. It is worth-mentioning that lists of basic goods of this kind very much resemble objective list theories. So, why a separate treatment now? My main reason does not have to do with foundation (appeal to self-evidence) or content (inclusion of religion or harmony with God in the list) but it is a reason of strategy. NNL has to be discussed and assessed in the course of the general discussion of natural law theory because its merits and faults are strictly connected with the position of the virtues within natural law.
88. Cf. W.E.May, "Contemporary Perspectives in Thomistic Natural Law" in J. Goyette, M .S. Latkovic, R. S. Myers (eds.), *ST. Thomas Aquinas and the Natural Law Tradition*, Catholic University of America Press, Washington, 2004, p 143.
89. Cf. A. Lisska, *Aquinas's Theory of the Natural Law: An Analytical Reconstruction*, Clarendon Press, Oxford, 1996, p. 156.
90. Cf. Finnis, *Aquinas*, Oxford University Press, Oxford, 1998, p. 80.
91. Cf. S.T. II-II q. 47 a.6c; q. 56 a.1c: these are the references quoted by Finnis.
92. Cf. Finnis, *Aquinas, cit.* pp. 83-4.
93. *Ibid.*
94. "A Virtue is to be valued precisely as one's actualizing the good of reasonableness." Finnis, *cit.*, p. 84n., referring to II-II q. 155 a.4 ad 3; Eth. IV. 9n 2.

95. Cf. Finnis, *cit.*, pp. 81-6.

96. Finnis, *Aquinas, cit.*, p. 105 n. 4.

97. *Ibid.*, p. 107.

98. CF. Finnis, NLNR, *cit.*, pp. 90-1-.

99. Cf. May, *Thomas Aquinas and the Natural Law Tradition*, Catholic University of America Press, Washington (DC), 2004, pp. 153-4.

100. G. Grisez, *The Way of Lord Jesus. Christian Moral Principles*, Vol. I, Franciscan Press, Quinci (Ill.) 1983, p. 192.

101. *Ibid.*, p. 184.

102. *Ibid.*, p. 192.

103. *Ibid.*, pp. 205-10.

104. *Ibid.*, p. 193.

105. *Ibid.*, p. 193-4.

106. Cfr. R. George, *Making Men Moral*, Oxford University Press, Oxford 1993, p. 19 ss; quoting I.Berlin, *The Crooked Timber of Humanity: Chapters in the History of Ideas*, Knopfl, New York, 1991.

107. *Ibid.*, pp. 38-9.

108. Cf. M. Nussbaum, "Virtue Ethics: A Misleading Category", *cit.*, p. 164 ff.

109. As Annas perspicuously notes "thought about the virtues, then, are self-effacing in the virtuous person." J. Annas, "The Phenomenology of Virtues", in *Phenomenology of Cognitive Science*, 7, 2008, p. 24.

Human Rights and Development: An Analysis with Special Concern to Environment

ARUN KUMAR SINGH*

INTRODUCTION

ALL human beings have the fundamental rights to an environment adequate for their health and well being. Nothing can be more fundamental than the issue of public safety and right to life .The right to life means not only to alive but to live with dignity, which also includes pollution free environment. Environment as defined, includes water, air, land and their interrelationship with human beings and other living organism. Society is a changing phenomenon which changes with the needs of craze for development. Scientific invention and high population resulted urbanization. Commercial pressure and rapid urban development resulted destruction of forests due to which ecological balance is being disturbed. Protection of environment in last few years became not only a matter of national concern but of international concern. It is sacred duty of every person to protect the nature and right to life together with environment, because environment provides life to everyone including mankind. Clean and wholesome environment is necessary for healthy living, hence clean and wholesome environment is an essential ingredient of right to life. The environment is very much affected with the development. Right to environment and right to development both are the human

*Assistant Professor, Department of Law, North -Eastern Hill University, Shillong-22.

rights of third generation. Every traditional human culture moves around the nature. Since the human beings learn everything from the nature. This paper aims to discuss the problems being faced by environment, impact of development over the environment national and international provisions regarding development and environment. It is also tried to highlight the role of Judiciary to protect the environment and to maintain balance between environment and development.

INTERNATIONALPROVISIONS

The treatments by the state of its nationals become matter of international concern. Conservation of environment and control of pollution become likewise a matter of international concern.[1] There occurs a process of internationalization of both human rights protection and environmental protection. Former begins from 1948 and later with the year of 1972, from Stockholm Declaration on the Human Environment.[2] India was also a participant and signatory of that conference. In the domain of environmental protection, it was reckoned that after certain activities the products like toxic or dangerous substance and radioactive elements, wastes may cause harmful effect to the environment. Actually the presence of dangerous substances became an issue on globalization level. After two year to Stockholm Conference, U.N. Charter on Economic Rights and Duties of states warned that the protection and preservation of the environment for present and future generation were the responsibility of the states.[3] In 1980 U.N. General Assembly proclaimed the historical responsibility of the state for the preservation of nature on behalf of the present or future generation.

Though Universal Declaration of Human Rights, 1948, has no direct reference to environment yet it reflects some conscience in respect of right to health and proper working environment.[4] In 1972, Stockholm Declaration on Human Environment expressly refers common goods to the mankind. This Declaration proclaimed that man is both creator and holder of environment which gives him physical sustenance and afford him the opportunity for intellectual and moral growth.[5] Paying respect towards human environment the Declaration provides that man has fundamental right to freedom, equality and adequate conditions of life in an environment of quality that permits a life of dignity and well being.[6] It also imposes duty to protect and improve the environment for present and future generation. The Stockholm Conference rejected the proposal for a 'Universal Declaration on the Protection and Betterment of the Environment' as a counter part of the U.N. Declaration of Human Rights.[7] It says that sovereign rights to exploit the natural sources should be in the conformity of the U.N. Charter. Besides that, Article 1(2), of the International Covenant on Civil and Political Rights corroborates the significance of environmental human rights.[8]' The Covenant further makes it logical saying that these are inherent rights and should not be impaired.[9]

The Rio Declaration on Environment and Development, 1992 also provides equality of opportunity for all in access to their basic resources, education, health services, food, housing and employment. The Declaration provides that human beings are the centre of concern for sustainable development and are therefore entitled to healthy and productive life in harmony with nature.[10]

The Vienna Declaration on Human Right, 1993 reiterates that the right to development should be fulfilled so as to meet equitably the developmental and environmental needs of present and of future generations.[11] It focused on the serious violation of human rights in the wake of incriminate proliferation of hazardous waste and pernicious dimension of science and technology. The Declaration considers the intergenerational equity and sustainable development in approach of right to life.

Apart from the above the first European Conference on Environmental Human Rights, (Strasburg) took place in 1979. The point was raised that the mankind needed to protect against its own threat to the environment, in particular when these threats had negative repercussions on the conditions of existence like life itself, physical and mental health and well being of present and future generations.

Besides the above, the United Nation is also concerned about the tribal's rights. It has realized that the existence of tribal people is under threatened. In this scenario the sensitivity has been shown by United Nation and provision has been made in the form of United Nation Declaration, 1948,[12] International Covenant On Civil and political Rights1966[13] International Covenant on Social Economic and Cultural rights1966,[14] United Nation Declaration on Racism and Racial Discrimination 1978,etc.[15]

NATIONAL PROVISIONS

Protection of environment can ensure life consistent with dignity and development of potential, because of an integral component of the rule of law. There are provisions for the protection of environment under the Article 47[16], 48 A[17]and 51 A (g) of the Constitution of India.[18] It also casts an obligation on the states as well as individuals to maintain and protect environment both man made as well as natural. *Post-Maneka* period witnessed an era of constitutional activism resulting into expanded interpretation of fundamental rights. As a result of highly creative interpretation right to healthy environment and many other rights has been included in the right to life guaranteed under Article 21 of the Constitution of India. Clean and wholesome environment is necessary for healthy living, hence clean and wholesome environment is an essential ingredient of right to life. Right to life together with environment becomes most important basic human right because environment provides life to everyone including mankind. Apart from the above provisions, there are other legislations to protect the environment. Forest Act of 1865 regulates forest exploitation management and preservation By this Act attempt was made to regulate the collection of forest produce by the forest dwellers. But the problem was that the Act was applicable only to the forest under the control of government and no provisions were made to cover private forest. Forest Act,1878, has more control over the forest because in this Act forests were divided into reserved forest protected forest and village forests. Indian Forest Act, 1927, strengthened forest department to regulate people's rights over the land. Forest Conservation Act, 1980, provides conservation of forest by checking indiscriminate diversion of forest land for non forest purposes. Apart from the above 1n 1980 a committee was appointed by the government of India known as the Committee on Forest and Tribal in India. The committee expressed that besides getting free fuel, fodder wood the tribal earn about one third of their income from the forest. The Committee also recommended that certain forest should be maintained as biosphere reserve. Besides above Protection of Environment Act, 1995 provides protection to the environment in various aspects. Apart from above Central Government considering the insecurity and rights of forest dwellers including those who were forced to relocate their dwelling due to development and state intervention passed an Act known as Traditional Forest Dwellers (Recognition of Forest Right) Act, 2006.[19]

ENVIRONMENTAL RIGHTS AND HUMAN RIGHTS

Before understanding the nature and scope of environmental rights it is essential to know the difference between human rights and environmental rights. Human rights are individual rights in the sense that beneficiaries are individual and are concerned with the protection of liberty, equality and freedom while environmental rights are collective rights. Whenever equality, liberty or freedom of an individual is violated it is violation of human rights. Environmental rights on the other hand relate to community entitlement or access to entitlement of community. Environmental rights are related with resources, conservation and long term sustainability. Consideration of socio-economic justice is more predominant than in the case of human rights where 'individualistic' facets of socio- economic justice are relevant. Despite that environmental rights are part of human rights in sense that they fulfill basic needs for survival of human being and healthy environment enable people to enjoy quality life which is guaranteed under Article 21 of the Constitution of India.

PROBLEMS REGARDING ENVIRONMENT

A healthy environment conducive to the health of human beings forms essential components of life.[20] Deforestation, over exploitation of natural sources, growing population, competition of development and pollution are causing adverse effect on environment. According to Paul Harrison.

'The final principle is respect for nature growth that does not respect the natural limits itself. Resources are exhausted, ecosystem collapse, species disappear and our own physical and mental health and even our survivals are threatened'.[21] There is great need to tackle problems like environmental degradation, pollution, deforestation climate change. Nature and its resources have their adequate capacity to feed and bear the burden of requirement of mankind.[22] Once these resources are overburdened due to the undue pressure of human activities, it disturb the equilibrium relationship between nature and mankind.[23] Consequently it gives rise to the problem of environmental pollution. Now people are facing serious problem of polluted air, polluted water, acid rains, global warming etc. The depletion of ozone layer causes skin cancer, cataract, and damage the body immunity. The main causes of environmental pollution are (i) Population explosion (ii) Over industrialization (iii) Unplanned urbanization (iv) Coal burnt thermal power generation (v) Poverty (vi) Deforestation (vii) An expansion in the use of efficient new technology with its associated demands on space food and natural resources.

Population Growth

The problem of population growth has become a global phenomenon which has got its alarming proportion in India. India have 2-4 per cent of global land but have second largest population in the world. Because of more population it puts heavy demand on natural resources like water, air, soil and forest. According to the study the tropical forest is shrinking by eleven million hectares a year.[24] Top soil is being lost at the rate of 26 billion tons in a year.[25] The problem of population has long been a very emotional issue because people require more food, land, housing and more water. For more food they use chemical fertilizers. Which is causing side effects to the people. The people also use insecticides, pesticides which resulted desert to the land and pollution causing harm to general people. Due to rapid growth of population people moving from villages to cities India is facing problem of urbanization.The problem of fast growth of mega cities is putting undue pressure on the basic necessities like sanitary, pure water, pollution free air etc. Number of vehicles are increasing due to which air pollution and noise pollution is increasing.

Over Industrialization

At present India is one of the most polluted countries because of over growth of industry. These Industries are increasing without proper regulation. Hazardous things and materials like oil, grease, petrochemicals are released from the industries and are coming in rivers. These materials make water unsightly and black. Delhi, Agra, Kanpur are the burning example of it. River *Yamuna* has lost its existence in Delhi, the water of the river is black and dirty. Same condition is in Agra. River *Ganga* is polluted in Kanpur. Chemicals present in industrial wastes making ground water acidic. Though many essential needs of human being are satisfied by the Industries, Industries extract raw materials from the nature and produce the products but at same time they pollute the environment.

Unplanned Urbanization

The cities in India are facing problems like shortage of sanitary lack of ventilated houses, lack of open spaces. The domestic waste disposal is serious problem in every city. Most of the area in cities have no sewer system. Apart from the above discharge of community wastage and industrial effluents are the major factor of water pollution.[26]

Deforestation

Forests protects land and water resources and produce oxygen for human being. They produce energy and wood products, medicine also. Because of extra use of woods, jungles are being cut. Due to which ecosystem is being disturbed. Deforestation is increasing carbon dioxides concentration on earth leading to global warming. According to the draft report of Inter Governmental Panel on Climate Change, given on February 16, 2007, sea levels will rise by at least 4cm by 2100, inundating vast areas on the coast line, including some of the most densely populated cities whose population will be forced to migrate inland or build dykes.[27] *Ganga, Bramhaputra* and *Indus* will be seasonal rivers. Water tables will continue to fall and gross per capita water availability in India be one third by 2050, as rivers dry up.[28] Water scarcity will in turn affect the health of vast populations with rise in water born disease. The temperature will rise up to 5.4 degree centigrade at the end of the century.[29]

Coal Burnt Thermal Power Plants

In India generally power plants use coal to generate electricity. This process results in the accumulation of various byproducts such as bottom ash, boiler slag and fly ash. Disposal of these ash is difficult and sensitive. The presence of ash particulars in the atmosphere is a major concern to the people living in close to the plant site. The finer fraction of fly ash are potentially harmful as they got deposited in lungs, pulmonary tissues of respiratory tracts when inhaled.

Use of New Technology

Man who is in quest for better quality of life and materialistic comfort have been exploiting and consuming resources at their command. Excessive exploitation of natural resources led to serious ecological crisis. That is why we need to search and develop environment friendly technology.

RIGHT TO DEVELOPMENT AND RIGHT TO ENVIRONMENT

Right to development as well as right to environment is the human rights of third generation. In recent years environmental concerns have become economic concerns. Neglect of environment in developmental policies and strategies of both the developed and developing countries has given rise to the serious global environment problem like ozone depletion, global warming, forest degradation and acid rain which not only threaten the very survival of earth and all those who live on it but also the fear about the sustainability of economic growth based on the present unsustainable patterns of production and consumption[30]. Awareness of the increasing vulnerability of the environment and the recognition and rapid and unabated degradation of the natural resources based on which economic activity and life itself may constitute the most serious threat to human well being [31]. Two issues have been particularly acute in recent negotiations: (i) Developing countries have sought to make their acceptance of environmental publications depending upon the provision of financial assistance and (ii) some developing countries in order to prevent competitive economic disadvantages have striven to ensure that environmental treaties establish effective institution which can verify and ensure that the contracting parties comply with their environmental obligations[32]. Article 1 of the United Nation Declaration on Right to Development defines right to development is an inalienable human right by virtue of which every human person and all peoples are entitled to participate, contribute and enjoy economic social cultural and political development in which all human rights and fundamental freedoms can be fully realized.[33] ECSOC established fifteen members working group of governmental experts. This working group was working on draft declaration on Right to Development submitted a text of preamble to the United Nation Commission on Human Rights on which general agreement reached, which stated; 'the human being is the central subject of the development policy which should have the human beings as the main participant and beneficiary of the development'[34].

It is further stated that the creation of condition favorable to the development of people and individual is the prime responsibility of the states. Development being basically a systematic positive phenomenon signifying not only the material welfare of people but also human value based on co-operation and non-exploitation requires a positive societal change. However the negative infraction between the development and natural resources has affected the environment adversely.[35] This puts a question before the basic relationship between the resource, people and the state.[36] Since development denotes a positive change in living conditions of the people but development should be scientific and systematic and not a hazard one.[37] The Stockholm declaration in linking environment with economic and social development acknowledges the fact that poverty forms the base for environmental problem in developing countries. The declaration enjoying the states to apply planning for developing human settlement and urbanization. Economic growth is *sin qna non* of any development model because this enables the community equal opportunity to fulfill its basic needs. Achieving harmony between the two can be the only way to attain meaningful development in India in presents situation. The industrial and technological advancements are necessary for the development, but it is true that modernization reduces the capacity of nature. Devastation are taking place in the forest, agricultural land, grazing land because of construction of dam, and urbanization. Though there is no alternative of development but balancing process has to be patronized between development and environmental concern. However, the Sustainable development has become the norm and new paradigm of future development process.

The concept of sustainable development contained in Stockholm Declaration of 1972.[38] Sustainable Development is a term which is subject to considerable interpretation depending upon the context of discussion and the audience of the debate. The World Commission on Environment and Development was created on the basis of Stockholm Conference. Mrs. Gro Harlem Burntland Chairman of the World Commission on Environment submitted a report, 'Our Common Future' in 1987 forwarded by Sri Rajiv Gandhi, the then Prime Minister of India. The report showed that politician industrialist and environmental groups around the world had endorsed sustainable development meeting the needs of present without compromising the ability of future generations to meet their own needs.[39] According to Laxman D. Guruswami, the concept of sustainable development involves at least two sets of contradiction. First, embedded in much of the sustainability thinking is an important difference of emphasis. Some view sustainability as a serious issue because nature is a major constraint on further human progress. They are concerned basically with the price paid by conventional growth model, if the warnings we receive from the environment are ignored, the biosphere will be destroyed. The solution, then, is to develop technologies, which avoid the direst environmental consequences of development or to take measures to assess environmental losses in a more realistic way. Indian Government has recognized the principle of sustainable development as basis for balancing ecological imperative with developmental goals.[40] To maintain balance between development and environment public trust doctrine should be followed. This doctrine emphasizes that the person will use natural resource as a trustee so that people of future generation can utilize the séance natural resource. It cannot be converted in to private ownership. It can be said that the constitutional obligation under Article 48 A[41] of the Constitution of India to protect and improve the environment bears close resemblance with this doctrine. Apart from this two other principles are there to protect the environment. They are polluter pays principles and precautionary principles. Polluter Pays Principle means polluter should internationalize the cost of their pollution control it and its sources and pay for its effects Polluter pays principle means that absolute liability for harm to the environment extends not only to compensate the victims of pollution but also the cost of restoring the environmental degradation[42].Polluter is liable to pay to the cost to the individual suffers as well as the cost of restoring the damaged ecology[43].This principle is adopted in India also. Precautionary Principles emphasizes that measures must anticipate, prevent and attack the causes of environmental degradation. Where there are threats of serious irreversible damage, lack of scientific certainty should be used for postponing measures to prevent environmental degradation. This is basically of foresees and assess environmental risk to worm potential victims of such risks and to behave in ways that prevent or mitigate such risks.

It is true that people are migrating from rural areas to cities and are mostly living in slums where no proper facilities of sanitary are available. They are running their shops and other businesses. Some time they cause pollution in that area in different ways. According to the government these slums create hindrance to the development project for modernizing the cities. That is why forced eviction of slums is taking place. However,United Nation Commission on Human Rights, prohibits forced eviction.[44] According to the Committee on Economic Social and Cultural Rights, forced eviction affects directly to the privacy of a person.[45] The Committee is of the view that eviction should not result in individual's homeless or vulnerable.The state party must provide adequate alternative housing, resettlement or access to productive land.[46] Despite that Indian position is quite different. For the sake of development people are forcibly evicted. Current examples of it are increasing the height of *Sardar Sarvoror* Dam, the incident of Harsood of Madhya Pradesh and Tata project of Nandigram district of West Bengal. In the above examples people are evicted from their own place, to other places which is gross violation of their human rights. Not only the violation of human rights of the people of the area where these projects are established but somehow it affects environment also. Unless proper rehabilitation and resettlement option is provided these people should not be evicted from their own places.

JUDICIAL RESPONSE

The right of everyone to a healthy environment entails duties incumbent upon everyone. Despite the existence of environmental policy, the constitutional mandate of environmental protection, flurry of legislation and administrative infrastructure the problem of environment is still remain a great cause of concern in India. Environmental consciousness has also rendered support to the demand of judicial activism in the field of environment. Article 142(1) of the Constitution has become a great source of inspiration to stress judicial activism. To meet the ends of justice the Article empowers Supreme Court to go beyond law and find out the habitation of justice.

In *Ratlam Municipality's case*[47] the Supreme Court has recognized the importance of pollution free environment and gave it the status of human right. In this case the Ratlam municipal town was popular with human and sub human species punctuated with affluence and indigence in contracting coexistence and keep public sanitation a low priority. The Supreme Court clarifies that public nuisance; because of pollution being discharged by big factories to the detriment of poor section is a challenge to the social justice component of rule of law. The Municipal Council which is constituted to preserve the health of public cannot run away from its duty by pleading financial crisis.

In *Subhash Kumar's case*[48] the fact in brief was that Subhash Kumar an influential businessman wanted to carry away slurry from the Tata Iron & Steel Company's ponds. Kumar tried various means to pressure the company into giving him business. When the company refused, he filed a public interest litigation under Article 32, claiming that the slurry discharged from the coal wateriest was polluting the Bokaro River and was a serious health risk to the neighbouring community. He asked the Court to prohibit TISCO's discharges. His interim application, however, revealed the real purpose: Kumar sought the Court's permission to carry away the slurry flowing into the river. Supreme Court has treated right to pollution free environment as integral part of right to life guaranteed by Article 21 of the Constitution of India. The Court observed Right to Life is a fundamental right under Article 21 of the Constitution and it includes the right to enjoyment of pollution free water and air for full enjoyment of life. If anything endangers or impairs the quality of life in derogation of laws, a citizen has right to have recourse to Article 32 of the Constitution for removing the pollution of water or air which may be detrimental to the quality of life.

In case of *Virendar Gaur v. State of Haryana* [49]The Court observed: Article 21 protects the right to life as fundamental right. Enjoyment of life including the right to live with human dignity encompasses within its ambit, the protection and preservation of environment without which life cannot be enjoyed.

The Supreme Court in case of *Vellore Citizens Welfare Forum v Union of India*[50] decided different issues relating to environmental protection under the principles adopted in Reo Declaration. A PIL was filed before Supreme Court under Art. 32 of the Constitution of India by a social action group, known as Vellore Citizen Forum to control environmental pollution caused by discharging of untreated effluents by the tanneries of Tamil Nadu to the river Palar which was the main source of water of that area. Tamil Nadu Agricultural University Research Centre, Vellore, after conducting a survey reported that around 35000 hectare of land in that area were affected for releasing the effluents and became unfertile. People of that area were facing the problem of drinking water. The Court considered the matter seriously and pointed out that development and ecology are opposed to each other is no longer acceptable. The Supreme Court directed the Centre to constitute an authority under section 3(3) of the Environment Protection Act with all necessary power to deal with situation created by the ternaries and other polluting industries in the state. A retired High Court Judge was placed at the head of new authority, which was to have a person with expertise in pollution control and environment protection as members. The authority was requested to identify the persons, who had suffered because of pollution, name the polluters liable to compensate the victims, assess the compensation to be paid and the cost of the remedial measures. The authority was asked to periodically review compliance by tanneries and to direct relocation of any industry where necessary[51].

Similarly in case of *T. Damodar Rao*[52] the writ petition has been filed by some of the residents of Hyderabad Municipal corporation who live around the above mentioned area to direct the municipal corporation to develop the entire area as residential area accordance with the approved development plan. A. P. High Court has rejected to grant permission to convert a portion of land for the construction of residential houses which was reserved for the purpose of park. The Court observed that enjoyment of life and the attainment and fulfillment as guaranteed by Article 21 of the Constitution embraces the protection and preservation of nature's gift without which life cannot be enjoyed. The slow poisoning by the polluted atmosphere caused by the environmental pollution and spoliation should be regarded as amounting to violation of article 21 of the Constitution. It therefore becomes legitimate duty of the Courts as the enforcing organ of the Constitutional objective to forbid all action of the state and the citizens from upsetting the environmental balance.

Apart from the above forgoing, there is also a question that can the right to livelihood be asserted to prevent environmentally disruptive project which threaten to uproot villagers and consequently deprive them of their livelihood? Supreme Court recognized the right to livelihood in the case of *Oliga Telis v. Bombay Municipal Corporation.*[53] Petitioner a journalist and two pavement dwellers challenged a government scheme to deport pavement dwellers from their place of origin. The main point of the argument was that the right to life includes right to livelihood, and the pavement dwellers would be deprived of their livelihood if they were evicted from their slums. Their eviction would be tantamount of deprivation of their life and was hence unconstitutional. The Court accepted the argument and held that deprive a person of his right to livelihood shall deprived him of his life. The state may not by affirmative action be compellable to provide adequate means of livelihood or work to citizen. But any person deprived of livelihood except according to just and fair procedure established by law, can challenged the deprivation as offending the right to life conferred by article 21 of the constitution.[54]

In *A.P. State Pollution Control Board v. M.V. Naidu*[55] Supreme Court once again observed that environmental concerns are in our view of equal importance as human rights. Both are to be traced to Article 21 which deals with fundamental right to life and liberty. Right to healthy environment and sustainable development are fundamental human rights implicit in the right to life. Right to life and right to environment are enshrined together.[56] Healthy environment enables people to enjoy a quality life which is the essence of guarantee under Article 21 of the Constitution of India.[57]

It is clear that protection of the environment is not only the duty of the citizens but also the obligation of the states and all other state organs including the Courts.[58] In that extent environmental law has succeeded in unshackling man's right to life and personnel liberty from the clutch of common law theory of individual's ownership. Examining the matter from the above constitutional point of view, it would be reasonable to hold that the enjoyment of life and its attainment and fulfillment guaranteed by article 21of the Constitution embraces the protection and preservation of nature's gift without which life cannot be enjoyed.[59] There can be no reason why practice of violent extinguishment of life alone should be regarded as violative of article 21 of the Constitution.[60] The slow poisoning by polluted atmosphere caused by environmental pollution and spoliation should be regarded as violation of article 21 of the constitution.[61] Sometime it is found that there is conflict between two human rights, in that case questions arises that which one will prevail? For example right to environment and right to development both are the parts of human rights. Can one be sacrificed for the other? In the case of *Rural Litigation and Entitlement Kendra Dehradun v. Uttar Pradesh*[62] the issue was in respect of the closure of certain limestone quarries in and around the town of the Mussoorie. The Court itself noted that the case was first of its kind in the country involving issues relating to environment and ecological balance and the questions arising for consideration were of grave moment and significance. The Court also noted that the situation involved in the conflict between development and conservation. It emphasized the need for reconciling the two in the larger interest of the country. The Court however avoided any discussion of the fundamental rights to a wholesome environment or its management from the guarantee of personal liberty. There is the small part of single sentence which refers to the need of safeguarding the rights of people to live in healthy environment with minimal disturbance of ecological balance and without hazard to them. The Court observed:

> "It is for the Government and the Nation and not for the Court to decide whether the deposits should be exploited at the cost of ecology and environmental considerations or the industrial requirement should be otherwise satisfied. It may be perhaps possible to exercise greater control and vigil over the operation and strike a balance between preservation and utilization; Government should take a policy decision and firmly implement the same. While the Court ordered in March 1985 the closure of some quarries, observed that this would cause hardship to the lessees but it is a price that has to be paid for protecting and safeguarding the right of the people to live in healthy environment with minimal disturbance of ecological balance and without avoidable hazard to them and to their cattle, homes and agricultural land and undue affectation of air, water and environment".

Thus, the Court gave precedence to a clean environment over the right to livelihood and development. The Court, however, required the Union of India "to balance these two aspects and place on record its stand not as a party to the litigation but as a protector of the environment in discharge of its statutory and social obligation.

Similarly Himachal Pradesh High Court in *Kinkri Devi v. State of Himachal Pradesh*[63] emphasized the need to strike a proper balance between industrial development and its adverse impact on ecology. The Court also ordered to review all the licenses granted for mining operation. The Court also held that industrial growth and exploitation of natural resources must proceed according to the norms mandate by the Constitution which is to preserve and improve the environment.

It is thus clear that industrial development and preservation of ecological balance must be harmonized. In *Indian Council for Enviro-legal Action v. Union of India*[64] the Apex Court observed that both development and environment must go hand in hand. In other word there should not be development at the cost of environment and *vice-versa,* but there should be development while taking due care and ensuring the protection of environment.

Animal and Indian Legal Defence fund v. Union of India[65] is a case where the Court observed that the rights of tribal's formerly living in the area to keep body and soul together must also receive proper consideration. From this observation the question arises that which one should be given priorities.

In case of *Sachchidanand Pandey v. State of West Bengal*[66] the land on which the hotel was to be constructed formerly belonged to the Alipore Zoological Garden and was put to important zoo-related uses. The zoo directors had withdrawn their objections to the hotel after the government promised them adjacent lands and relocation grants, and the hoteliers agreed to reconstruct all displaced facilities on the adjacent lands, at no expense to the zoo. The Court referred Article 51A (g) of the Constitution that it is the Fundamental duty of every citizen of India to protect and improve the natural environment. The Court held that, when the Court is called upon to give effect to the Directive Principle of State Policy and the Fundamental Duty, the Court is not to shrug its shoulder and say that priorities are a matter of policy and is a matter of policy making authority. At least the Court may do it to examine whether appropriate consideration are born in mind and irrelevant are excluded. The Supreme Court in this case has reminded the government and citizens of their social obligation to preserve and maintain the ecological balance.

In *Ganga Pollution Case*[67] the Court followed the strategy of Pandey's case. The brief fact of the case is that M.C. Mehta an activist, social worker filed a writ petition by way of public interest litigation under Article 32 of the Constitution for the issue of writ order/direction in the nature of *mandamus* directing Kanpur Municipality to restrain from letting out trade effluents into the river Ganga till such time that they put up necessary treatment plants for treating the trade effluents in order to arrest the pollutants. The respondents allege that effluents are first discharged into the Municipal sewer; hence they are not under an obligation to set up treatment. Overriding this vague contention the Supreme Court held that the fact that the effluents are first discharged into Municipal sewers did not absolve the tanneries being proceeded against the provisions of the law enforced since the effluents reach to the Ganga river from Municipal sewers. The Supreme Court held that the financial inabilities are no excuse for letting the untreated sewage or material hazardous to public health in the environment.

Apart from the above in case of *M. C. Mehta v. Kamalnath*[68] in 1995, Span Motels built a resort on the bank of the Beas River between Kullu and Manali in Himachal Pradesh. Kamal Nath, formerly the Union Minister of Environment and Forests, had links to the hotelier, who had encroached a swathe of forest land. The encroachment was 'validated' in 1993-94, during Nath's tenure as minister. During the 1995 monsoons, the river engulfed part of the land and threatened the resort. In an effort to protect its property, both before and after the 1995 floods, span motels carried out substantial work (dredging, construction of concrete barriers, wire crates, etc.) to deflect the flow of river. The Supreme Court held that in order to protect life, in order to protect environment, and in order to protect air, water and soil from pollution, this Court in its various judgments has given effects to the rights available to the citizens and the persons alike, under Article 21 of the Constitution. The state is the trustee of all natural resources which are by nature meant for public use and enjoyment. The public at large is the beneficiary of the sea-shore, running waters, air, forests and ecologically fragile lands. These resources cannot be converted into private ownership.

The Supreme Court in *K.M. Chinappa v. Union of India*[69] stated that, the enjoyment of life and its attainment including their right to life with human dignity encompasses within its ambit the protection and preservation of environment, ecological balance free from pollution of air and water, sanitation without which life cannot be enjoyed. Hygienic environment is thus integral part of healthy life. Right to live with human dignity becomes illusory in absence of human and healthy environment.

Similarly in *Madhya Pradesh v. Kedia Leather and Liquor Ltd.*[70] Supreme Court held that right to pollution free environment also includes the right to enjoyment of pollution free water and air for full enjoyment of life. Once again Supreme Court emphasizes the proper utilization of natural sources. According to the Court the natural resources of air, water and soil cannot be utilised if the utilization results in irreversible damage to environment.[71]

In *Tehri Bandh Virodhi Sangharsh Samiti v. State of Uttar Pradesh*[72], the rivers Bhagirathi and Bhilangana rise in the Garhwal Himalayas in north-western Uttar Pradesh and flow south to the plains as the Ganga. As part of a larger plan to trap the waters of the Upper Ganga basin, a three billion dollar clay core, rock fill dam is being constructed at the confluence of Bhagirathi and Bhilangana, close to the Garhwal town of Tehri. The lake created by the dam will extend upto 45 kms in the Bhagirathi Valley and 25 kms in the Bhilangana Valley with a water spread area of 42.5 sq. Kms. It will submerge nearly 100 villages, including Tehri, a historical capital. As many as 85,600 families will be relocated as a result. On the benefits side of the equation, the project is supposed to generate 2,400 MW of electricity, create irrigation facilities for 270,000 hectares of land, and create a supply of 500 cusecs of water to New Delhi. The Tehri dam project has provoked controversy focused on three issues. The completed dam will displace many people and submerge several towns, among them the town of Tehri; the region is vulnerable to earthquakes and the dam may be structurally incapable of withstanding them or may perhaps even cause them; and the possible failure of the dam could kill hundreds of thousands of people and destroy downstream towns of immense religious significance. Of particular concern are the 170,000 inhabitants of the downstream Hindu holy towns of Hardwar and Rishikesh. Both the resettlement policies and the structural flaws of the dam have provoked civil protests, lawsuits and international attention that have repeatedly stalled the project which was begun in 1978. The Tehri project was challenged in the Supreme Court in a writ petition filed by the Tehri Bandh Virodhi Sangharsh Samiti in 1985. The Supreme Court dismissed the petition in 1990 after a very limited enquiry. Although the Environmental Appraisal Committee had unanimously concluded that the Tehri project should not be approved, the Central Government relied instead on an opinion of the Department of Mines to convince itself and the Court that the project was sound.

CONCLUSION

The evolution of man as social being began in small group of communities who were struggling for the existence. This struggle was regarding the natural resources. *Adivasies* are the decedents of these early settlers. These people has played important role in different areas such as development of traditional herbal medicine, contribution to the modern art and craft and preservation of biodiversity etc. These people together nature maintain cycle of the nature. But in this phenomenon nature is directly are indirectly affected. The right to life with dignity is recognized in fundamental right under Article 21 of the Constitution of India. It is the inherent right not a gift of law and is closely related with the environment. But the environment is facing some problems. These problems are of two categories. Those which are the negative effects of the development and those which result from poverty and under development. Improper planning of development deprives those who are directly affected by the development. Large scale of displacement and pollution are the example of it. Though National Human Right Commission recommended that suitable legislation should be made for the rehabilitation to the people who are going to be displaced. Proper planning for the development is necessary because by the displacement their privacy as well as livelihood is affected. There is need to set up independent national agency to act as watching dog to prevent abuse and over exploitation of natural resource particularly in forest areas. Tribes who have traditional rights on forest and dependent upon them, must be protected from commercial exploitation by outsiders. Apart from this sustainable development must be clearly defined so that it can be enforced by law.

Thus from the above discussion it is clear that right to safe environment is implicit in Article 21 of the Constitution. Higher Judiciary in its judicial invention and creativity removed the anonymity by reading the wholesome environment in the right to life as penumbral right. The judicial pronouncement reflects the Courts approach balancing the value of development and environment protection. The Supreme Court has always upheld the preciousness of environment not by choice but being need of situations. Judicial verdicts have given appropriate dimension to the development of environmental jurisprudence. The governing norms as proclaimed by agenda 21, should be integration of imperative with development aspirations.

However, the penalties for violation of environmental law are weak in India. The Environmental (Protection) Act, 1986 and other relative measures have provisions for penalties. But sometime judiciary interferes in it and weakens the provisions of penalties. The Indian legislative measure for ozone depletion has been enacted in the year 2000, is not so effective because lacks in developing judicial response and other legislative measures to deal with problem of global environmental change. Therefore some attention is required for making the environmental law effective. The judiciary is also required to have concern for curbing the problem of environment because there is urgent need to regulate the consumption and exploitation of natural sources in a sustainable manner. To avoid the problem of ozone depletion there are many initiatives which the country can adopt to reduce carbon emissions without sacrificing its priority of economic development. Oil and Gas are the fastest growing segments of our energy basket and we should maximize their availability to run our economy. [73] If the railway system is fully electrified and railway offers satisfactory service a big reduction in oil use will take place. All metro cities must have metro system then there will be reduction of carbon emission. Magnetic levitation would greatly increase the efficiency in electric traction.

Notes

1. Antonio Augugusto Concado Trindade 'Human Rights and the Environment' in Janusz Symonides *New Dimension and Challenges for Human Rights*, 2003, New Delhi, Rawat Publication, p. 118.
2. *Ibid.*
3. Article 30 of the Stockholm Declaration, 1972.
4. Article 25 of the Declaration 1948, says 'everyone has the right to standard of living adequate for the health and welding of himself and for his family including food clothing housing, medical care and necessary services'.
5. Principle 1, United Nation Declaration on Human Environment, 1972.
6. *Ibid.*
7. Md. Zafar Mahfooz Nomani 'Human Right to Environment in India: from Legality to Reality'. *Delhi law Review*, Vol. XXII, 2000, p. 85.
8. Article 1(2) of International Covenant on Civil and Political rights says 'All people may for their any ends freely dispose of their natural wealth and sources without prejudice to any obligation arising out of international co-operation based upon the principle natural benefits. In no case a people be deprived its own means of subsistence.
9. Article 25 of International Covenant on Civil and Political Rights states that nothing in the present covenant shall interpreted as impairing the inherent right of all people to enjoy and utilize fully and freely their natural wealth and resources.
10. Article 1 of the Reo Declaration on Environment and Development, 1992.
11. Article 11 of Vienna Declaration and Programme of Action on World Conference on Human Right (A/Cong. 157/24, 25 June) 1993.
12. Article 17 of the Declaration provides that everyone has the right to own the property alone as well as in association with others and that no one shall be arbitrarily deprived of his property. Though this recognizes common rights of property, it is predominantly in terms of the individual's occupation and access to the property and does not explicitly cover the common property of group people.
13. Article 27 of the Covenant provides stipulates that in those states in which ethnic religious or linguistic minorities exists, persons belonging to such minorities shall not be denied the rights in the community with other member of the group to enjoy their own culture to profess and practice their own religion or to use their language.

14. Article1 of the conventions provides that all people have the rights to self determination. By virtue of that right the feely determine their political status and freely pursue their economic social and political development. See also Article 1 of the International Covenant on Civil and Political Rights, 1 1966.

15. ICJ Report, October1975reveals that tribal people have right to maintain their traditional structure of economy and culture and stress that their land, land rights and natural resources should not be taken away from them.

16. Article 47 provides, "the state shall regard the raising of level of nutrition and the standard of living of its people and the improvement of public health as among its primary duties and in particular the state shall endeavor to bring about prohibition of consumption except for medical purposes of intoxicating drinks and of drugs which are injurious to health".

17. Article 48 A provides, "the state shall endeavor to protect and improve the environment and to safe guard the forest and wild life of the country."

18. Article 51 A (g)provides, "it shall be the duty of every citizen of India to protect and improve the natural environment including forest, lakes, river and wild life and to have compassion of all living creatures".

19. The object of the Act is (i) to recognize and visit forest rights and occupation in forest land in forest dwelling scheduled tribes and other traditional forest dwellers who have been residing in such forests for generations but whose rights to be rewarded.

    (ii) to recognize the rights of forest dwelling scheduled tribes and other forest dwellers include responsibility ssssand authority for sustainable use conservations of ecological balance.

    (iii) to do away with the injustice done to the tribal people and to give them back their esteemed rights.

20. J. S. Verma, *The New Universe of Human Rights* 2004, Delhi, Universal Law Publishing Co. Ltd., p. 168.

21. Paul Harrison, Third World Tomorrow 1991 at 345 in G. S. Tiwari, 'Developing Jurisprudence of Principle Environmental Protection and Environmental Rights', *NationalCapital Law Journal*, 2004 IX p. 27.

22. Dr. K. C. Jena 'Environmental Pollution and its Legal Control in India', in AIR2000 (J) p. 178.

23. *Ibid.*

24. *Ibid.*

25. *Ibid.*

26. *Ibid.*

27. Daphne Wysham and Smitu Kothari, 'Climate change will devastate India', *The Hindu* 9th April 2007 p. 11.

28. *Ibid.*

29 *Ibid.*

30. B. C. Nirmal 'From Vellore to Nayadu: The Customary Law status of the Precautionary Principle, *The Banaras Law Journal,* Vol. 30, 2001. p. 58.

31. *Ibid.*

32. R. A. Malviya, 'Issues, Concepts and Definitions in International Environmental Law: New Perspectives', in *The Banaras Law Journal,* Vol. 30, 2001, p. 51.

33. U. N. G. A. Resolution 4/128 of 4 December 1986.

34 U.N. DOCE/CN 4/1985/ II dated Jan 24, 1985 at para 12.

35. Vijay Kumar 'Environmental Poverty Development and the State in Perspective of less Developed Countries' in *Delhi Law Review,* Vol. XXVI, 2004, p. 56.

36 *Ibid.*

37 *Ibid.*

38. U. N. Conference on the Human Environment was held at Stockholm from 5-16 June 1972 to tackle the global problem of protection and improvement of the human environment by International Consensus. About 114 nations participated there. The principle decisions, resolutions and recommendations of the conference were as follows:

    1. A resolution in plenary session condemning nuclear weapons test, especially those carried out in the atmosphere and calling on the states intending to carry out such test to refrain from doing so, as these might lead to further contamination of the environment.

    2. A unanimous recommendation that world environment day be observed on 5 June each year.

    3. An Action Plan for protection and enhancement of the environment was enforced, which had three parts:

        (i) earth watch programme to identify problems of International significance so as to warn against environmental crisis.

        (ii) recommendation concerning environmental management i.e. what was necessary to manage the environment and

(iii) supporting measures such as education, training public information and finance.

4. The adoption of the Declaration of the Human Environment ,which may be regarded as doing for the protection of the environment of the earth what the Universal Declaration of Human rights of 1948 accomplished for the protection of fundamental freedoms and human rights.

5. Recommendation were made to the United Nation General Assembly for the creation of new International machinery.

6. Recommendation for establishing voluntary environmental fund.

7. It was recommended that the General Assembly should decide to convene a second United Nation conference on Human Environment.

In Principle 21 and 22 of the Declaration on Human Environment three principles of International Law were proclaimed.

(i) States have a sovereign rights to exploit policies.

(ii) States are responsible for ensuring that the activities within their jurisdiction control do not cause damage to the environment of other states or areas beyond the limits of national Jurisdiction.

(iii) State are under a duty to co-operate to develop further the International Laws as liability and compensation for the victims of pollution.

39. See also World Commission on Environment and Development "Our Common Future" (1990)

40. Divan, Rosencrenz, *Environmental Law and Policy in India 2003,*Delhi Universal Law Publishing Co. Ltd. p. 585.

41. Article 48 A, Provides that the State shall endeavor to protect and improve the environment and to safeguard the forest and wild life of the country.

42. Jai Jai Ram Upadhyay *Environmental Law,* 2005, Allahabad, Central Law Agency, p. 137.

43. *Ibid*

44. According to U. N. Commission on Human rights, Resolution 1993/ 77 forced eviction constitutes a gross violation of human rights.

45. Committee on Economic social and Cultural rights, General Comment 7 Forced Evection and Rights to Adequate Housing (sixteenth session, 1997) U.N. Doc./ 1998, para 1.

46. *Ibid* at para 16.
47. *Municipal Council, Ratlam v. Virdi Chand,* AIR 1980 SC 1622.
48. *Subhash Kumar v. State of Bihar,* AIR 1991 SC 420.
49. 1995 (2) SCC 577.
50. AIR 1996 SC 2715.
51. *Ibid.*
52. *Damodar Rao v. S.O. Municipal Corporation, Hyderabad,* AIR 1987 AP 171.
53. AIR 1986 SC 180.
54. *Ibid.*, p. 194.
55. AIR 1999 SC 812
56. *Narmada Bachao Andolan v. Union of India* (2000) 10 SCC.
57. *Hinch Lal Tiwari v. Kamala Devi* (2001) 6 SCC 496.
58. Shyam Divan, Armin Rosencranz, *Environmental Law and Policy in India* 2005, New Delhi, Oxford University Press, p. 389.
59. *Ibid.*
60. *Ibid.*
61. *Ibid.*
62. AIR 1985 SC 652.
63. AIR 1998 H.P. at 4
64. JT (1996) (4) SC 263.
65. JT (1997) (3) SC 298.
66. AIR 1987 SC 1109.
67. AIR1988 SC 1037
68. (2000) 6 SCC 213
69. AIR 2003 SC 724 p. 731
70. (2003) 7 SCC 398 p. 394
71. *M.C. Mehta v. Union of India* 2004(2) SCALE, 683
72. 1992 Supp. (1) SCR 44.
73. M. R. Srinivasan, 'Climate Change and India's Option', *'The Hindu'*, 30th June 2007 p. 12.

Finding Footing in a Postmodern Conception of Law

Bryan Druzin*

INTRODUCTION

To what extent are the basic principles that underlie our legal system universal? To what extent do they follow the dictates of human reason and appeal to an intuitive sense of what is fair, and are not simply the products of specific historical, economic, and cultural circumstances? If one believes they are in fact universal in character, one would expect to find general symmetry between the concepts that gird our legal systems. Criminal codes between legal cultures should mirror one another, as should other areas of law ranging from family law to constitutional law. The law of tort, for instance, where the chief aim is *restitutio in integrum*,[1] namely a remedy that is fair to all parties involved, a body of law founded upon an intrinsic sense of fairness applied to the mundane particularities of human interaction—should likewise exhibit homogeny between legal cultures.

Yet, we do not find this degree of uniformity.[2] Legal conceptions of what is fair are not always identical between legal systems, influenced significantly by religious, cultural, and arguably, economic factors. Not only do understandings of fair play sometimes differ between legal systems, even within a single unified system of law, such as the English common law, the concepts that underlie the law have changed over time. Wholly

*Attorney at Law and PhD Candidate and Lecturer at King's College London.

new principles, such as criminal insanity and negligence have been introduced. The law has transformed significantly over time, adapting to the trappings of its historical age. Conceptions of nuisance, trespass to land, and trespass to chattels have evolved in a fashion that seems inseparable from principles of private property and economic necessity—concepts integrally linked to specific economic systems such as capitalism.[3] Many areas of tort such as economic torts are explicitly connected to certain economic positions that have emerged over time. This includes areas such as consumer protection, product liability, and restraint of trade. Even damages for intangible losses such as pain and suffering in the form of pure mental anguish reflect a certain cultural perspective. Family law, commercial law, and criminal law have all similarly undergone varying degrees of transformation. Thus, we do not find a static view of fairness as defined by law; rather, we have a shifting body of conceptions, in a state of subtle flux, continually experiencing change in reaction to general shifts in cultural attitudes.

What then are we left with when we consider the possibility that these legal principles are not extracted from immutable natural truths, but rather are largely subjective concoctions of the cultures that formulate them, specific to the values of that particular age? It is, in a sense, frightening. It strikes at the very heart of our sense of justice. It seems that upon the shifting sands of postmodern moral relativism, there is no firm footing on which to stand. So what are we left with? Does not the denial of objective truth ultimately undercut the premise that there is objective value -the very notion of justice? Are we left with only the prospect of uncertainty and moral anarchy? Is this Nihilism?[4] The argument of postmodernism is a powerful one. Its implications are profound, and thus, we must address it. This short paper will do just that, suggesting that, despite the absolute, all-consuming nihilism towards which postmodernism seems to lead in its most extreme form, the acceptance of postmodern relativism in fact in no way undermines the possibility of finding firm footing on which to stand, of finding moral certainty, and thus solid ground for our legal principles. To do this, the discussion that follows detours significantly from the conventional route of a law paper; I ask for the reader's patience in travelling this circuitous path through the terrain of philosophy. Notwithstanding this, however, the discussion's final destination indeed directly addresses the very foundations upon which our conceptions of law are typically constructed, the heart of law—our sense of what is just.

THE JETTISING OF OBEJCTIVE MORAL TRUTH

Subjectivity in the Law

To an extent, we already tacitly acknowledge a degree of moral relativism in the law. We establish legal standards to govern our society presumably founded upon moral imperatives, yet readily accept the validity of quite different legal standards within other cultures. I say to an extent because if the difference is too extreme, too egregious, we do not accept it. However, it is remarkable how high the threshold actually is for this measure of acceptance. It is astonishing how easily we can simply chalk the disparity up to a simple difference in cultural mores.

The age for sexual consent is a good example. In many jurisdictions the age is eighteen. However the age of consent under Danish law is fifteen.[5] While an adult engaging in sexual relations with a 15 year-old in the United States would be convicted of child molestation and seen generally by society as a paedophile, the exact same scenario would be tolerated by Danish society. And although this is the case, the rest of the world does not view the Danish legal system as sanctioning child molestation. But why not? How can this conform to the idea that our laws related to an issue of such importance as child molestation are grounded upon universal moral truths? Should not most Americans logically view Danish society as endorsing child molestation? Similarly, as British, French, German, Italian, Australian and Canadian law prohibits the use of execution in their respective legal systems, should these judiciaries, in the spirit of the law, not then view most U.S. nationals as being accessories to murder?[6] The Canadian Criminal Code, for instance, provides "that every one is a party to an offense who: does or omits to do anything for the purpose of aiding any person to commit it; or abets any person in committing."[7] Is not the whole of American society then culpable in that they fail to change these laws? The answer of course is no, and the mere mention of the idea seems absurd, as we feel each society is free to establish laws that are in line with their own moral standards. But again, how can this be reconciled with our notion that there is a fixed moral underpinning to the laws we enact? Clearly, we do tacitly acknowledge a degree of moral subjectivity beyond mere technical issues of jurisdiction. This is the deeper issue at play within the area of Conflicts of Law. On a purely practical level, our legal system often collides with other systems of law predicated on slightly differing notions of right and wrong. National laws at variance bring the issue of relativism to the fore in stark clarity.

Legal Positivism

Perhaps, it was as a result of a growing realization of the palpable disparity between our systems of law in the area of Conflicts of Law that legal positivism appeared within the margins of late nineteenth and early twentieth century jurisprudence, eventually replacing earlier natural law notions that held law as inextricably linked with a basic sense of justice and yes, morality. This separation of law and ethics is profoundly significant. With it, one could simply divorce law from morality, and leave legal regulation as a shallow vessel of legal positivism, bereft of ethical significance. One could bark out the separation thesis as espoused by many legal positivists, the idea that legal validity has no inherent connection with morality or a conception of justice, and be done with it.[8] However, anything short of absolute postmodern relativism must ultimately be grounded upon some form of overarching justification for a given system of law, be it some form of natural law, class struggle, or simple utilitarianism—there must be an underlying sense that it is correct and justified. Without this sense, *why then would we even need to have it?* Does not the fact that we still find it necessary to institute laws imply that there is an underlying justification and that this rationale is predicated on some semblance of objective truth offering at the minimum, pragmatic guidance if not moral direction?

Legal positivism, however, we should remember, is not wholly removed from an underlying idea of social control, or that maintaining a certain societal order, or simply the notion that staving off anarchy is a 'good thing.'[9] In a sense it replaces one rationale with another. But all rationales must be grounded upon an overarching notion of what is 'good' (for lack of a better word). Without this, the whole construction crumbles.[10] Carried to its extreme, the postmodern position, however, scratches mercilessly at this wound, thus threatening to undermine all possible constructions regardless of its rationale, by obliterating the idea of objective truth itself. Legal positivism, to be sure, is singularly important in that it is a stepping-stone towards the metastasising of postmodern thought within law. By snapping the tether that, for hundreds of years (arguably throughout all of human history), bound law to an underlying bedrock of moral justice, it opens the door towards absolute relativism, and leaves us with a fundamental problem yet to be resolved: if law is not morality, what is it? Is the concept of justice, the shared human recognition of fairness –a grandiose historical myth? What is it, a social construction, a hastily written provision in our social contract, an internalised norm[11] born form an adaptive quality? To use a legal turn of phrase, the floodgates open.

Critical Legal Studies

The idea that there exists a relativist quality to law lingering just beneath our formalistic assumptions is expressed in the Critical Legal Studies (CLS) movement which emerged in the 1970s and 1980s as an independent subset of legal theory.[12] Influenced significantly by the ideas of the Frankfurt school (with the exception of Habermas) and French poststructuralism, CLS strove to expose as arbitrary the received social and political beliefs that underlie and shape our systems of law.[13]

Postmodern theorists, also known as "anti-foundationalists" and "critical legal students," claim "the law cannot have any foundation because there is no foundation for objective knowledge of any kind. They say we cannot objectively understand reality because all knowledge is contingent on social convention (especially language)."[14] Thus, there are no foundational principles upon which to position the edifice of law. "Principles of law" these theorists go on to conclude "could never reflect universal truths . . . only allocations of power among social groups. According to these scholars, it is senseless to talk about whether a law is right or wrong or moral or amoral. Law is whatever the most powerful cultural group in society makes it."[15] Indeed, in the CLS perspective of law, all legal "truths" are mere mental constructs shaped by social convention. CLS boldly contends that objective ethical truth is a fiction, thus "consensus within a viable community is all we mean by the truth of ethical propositions . . ."[16] CLS theorists pointedly reject the notion that there is "good," or objective morality.[17] We are instead confronted by the subjective, cultural constructions that society erects to stand like ethical fortifications for us to retreat inside. Ultimately, anti-foundationalist theorists argue, these fortifications are arbitrary creations built upon a foundation of sand, the search for objective truth "misguided."[18]

The Flux of Mere Opinions

So how deep does this go? The postmodern method of deconstruction begins like peeling an onion. Layer after layer is pulled away to see what lies underneath, and layer by layer the onion is made smaller, until eventually one is left with only its empty core—nothing. Carried to its extreme, postmodernism deconstructs the very foundations on which the possibility of ever arriving at truth with a capital 'T' is built. Indeed, it puts forward the proposition that truth in this sense does not exist, that there is never indeed anything true apart from the values that arise from our own subjective constructions, or in the terminology of Foucault, that we create entire belief structures through the 'discourses' through which we engage the world.[19] Apart from the very process itself of creating value, there does not exist any objective truth.

It is important for us to be clear; it is not that we can never achieve objectivity, but rather the whole notion of objectivity itself is an unreal concept. It is a figment of our imagination. It simply does not, nor ever has existed. This is not the denial of things in themselves. It is not solipsism.[20] No one is saying the chair is not there, or that fire does not burn. Rather, it is a complete denial of the objective validity of the value systems we construct around the external world. That is, the views that proliferate in relation to the objective world. Thus, as there is no 'real' in this sense, there is simply no hope of objectivity, only perspective. All we can ever know is one particular view as an alternative for another. And we are forever swimming in these perceptions. Whatever perspective the individual or culture engages in, takes on the illusion of truth for that individual or culture.

In a sense, one could argue that the very concept of truth is a by-product of view. Let us examine this idea by way of illustration

cold, starvation, or even our fear of death? Equally, why should we not question our love of warmth, food, security, power, and beauty? To imagine these things may be totally arbitrary seems grossly counter-intuitive. They appear to be extracted from indelible truths prescribed by nature itself. One would of course reply that Bartley's fear is unfounded as nothing 'harmful' would result from contact with unwashed grapes, while our fear of cold is rational because our bodies may become sick as a result of overexposure to cold. But we must not stop here, let us keep going. Well, if the body becomes sick, it may cease functioning. If it ceases functioning, we may die. And...if we die, this is a bad thing. And so there we have it: indisputable truth.

However, we must follow our analysis to its inevitable conclusion. How is the human fear of death itself unlike Bartley's fear of unwashed grapes? How is it any less arbitrary? Is it not only because these value determinations are so deeply embedded into our psyche, so necessitated by our physical state, and so pervasive and commonly held, that they seem beyond question—that they appear to us to possess categorical objectivity? These are value assumptions so entrenched into the nature of being alive, that it is inconceivable that, at the end of the day, they are not rooted in the real. And yet, they are not. If we could step beyond these patterns of belief that bind us to the blind acceptance that our values are self-evident truths, we would see clearly that, in the final analysis, our value system is wholly relative and no less arbitrary than Bartley's. But to put it mildly, this is a difficult thing to do. In fact, it is a virtually impossible thing to do, and our very inability to grasp this reality, speaks to how deeply rooted and powerful these perceptions really are. There is no difference between any of us and Bartley. All value is constructed, not intrinsic. Indeed the entire edifice of value itself - of any sense of value - is just the equivalent of unwashed grapes.

Bartley and Death by Vehicular Idiocy

Let us take another example involving Bartley, again illustrating the same point. In an effort to alleviate some of the anxiety brought about by his debilitating condition, Bartley's therapist recommends he take a vacation. Putting aside his paralysing fear of unwashed grapes, Bartley takes his trusted doctor's advice and takes a trip to

London, England. He rents a car and plans a route through the English countryside, careful to avoid the few wineries that operate in the UK. As Bartley winds his way over the empty country roads of rural England, finally free of the oppressive terror of unhygienic grapes, he notices a tractor-trailer heading directly towards him. The massive truck is driving on the same side of the road as Bartley and refusing to change lanes. Bartley is bewildered. As Bartley frantically sounds his horn, the horn of the truck blares back at him, and the truck continues to barrel towards poor Bartley. Bartley panics yet again wishing he had never left home. And just at the point of impact, as Bartley's small car is about to be utterly crushed by the tractor trailer, we still the frame and notice (of course) that Bartley is driving on the right side of the road.

Clearly, if you will, we have here two conflicting value systems: a value system that deems driving on the right side of the road as correct and one that posits the left side of the road as correct. This highlights the postmodern dilemma in distinct terms. Driving on the right side of road is no more inherently valid than driving on the left. Certainly, this practice of driving on one side of the road or the other is no more than a mere cultural phenomenon, having no objective claim to being any truer than any other. What we have here are rules completely unrelated to any moral framework –a set of norms that show themselves as utterly subjective social constructions. That is fine enough, but what are we to tell Bartley who is about to be killed by oncoming traffic? Does it make a wit of difference? The rules do not have any objective reality to them in the sense that they are not grounded on any universal truth; however, the result (his impending death) is very real. That is to say, is there any question that traffic rules are arbitrary? But of what use is this insight when you are hit by a truck? If a man takes it upon himself (unlike Bartley) to intentionally drive on the right side of the road in a place where the rules dictate that traffic must drive on the left, is it not then a moral issue? People are going to get hurt; it does not matter that the rules are not founded upon objective truth. In a very real sense, they have become objective truths.

Pain and Moral Clarity

Let us now return to poor Bartley in the first example. How could subjecting this man to unwashed grapes be morally wrong? Let us get to the heart of the matter. It is wrong because in doing so we would cause Bartley to suffer, and it is precisely human suffering that is the yardstick with which to gauge right from wrong -the core underpinning to justice. Indeed, it is, and always has been, the only process through which 'good' is defined; the whole of morality is grounded upon the extent to which an act creates suffering and the extent to which the act reduces suffering. This is all morality ever is. Although it may flower into systems of ethical complexity, it remains nothing more than just this. All sense of value is ultimately contingent upon this experience, and evolves from it. The experience of suffering be it physical or mental, is the very definition of "negative." *Negative has no meaning beyond this.*[23] "Negative" is the experience of suffering, and its inverse, 'positive', is the cessation of this very same sense of suffering. It is a self-defining process that in no uncertain terms "reifies" itself. Once it is ushered into existence, it is "real." The experience of suffering is the root of good and bad. It is its very core. Put simply, it is not the basis of right and wrong, it is the progenitor of right and wrong. Value is never anything more than the sum total of suffering and the lack of it. Human suffering is not the defining factor of value; it is not a mechanism through which to measure value—*it is value.*

An act in itself has no implicit moral character. It is the occurrence of suffering that provides a moral context through which an act becomes either right or wrong. To illustrate this point, let us return then to the question raised above regarding slavery. Imagine a situation in which the institution of slavery did not in any way create even a trace of human suffering— a situation where the slave did not experience pain (physical or emotional) as a result of his bondage. Even the master was not morally corrupted by this exploitive relationship, and does not mentally suffer as a result of his cruelty. Certainly, this kind of situation is not possible, but for argument's sake, let us suppose this is the case—absolutely no suffering is created for any parties, directly or otherwise. How could we then say that this situation is morally wrong? We could not. Once the element of suffering is taken out of the equation, the physical act of slavery ceases to possess any moral significance.[24] This does not seem to gel with our fundamental notions of right and wrong. It is, however, only because we intuitively recognize that this situation could never truly arise, that it appears so patently wrong. It is because we are aware that slavery as an institution is the cause of such misery that it is morally repugnant to us. However, let us not confuse the issue; it is not the act of slavery itself, it is the suffering it creates. The element of pain once introduced upon our emotional landscape imbues the world with a measure of moral reality. We construct entire value systems within which we then live, but the moment we react to these constructions, all subjectivity ends. Our reactions are real. There is good and bad, right and wrong.

It is important to understand that what is being denied here is not that our belief systems and sense of value are largely determined by culture, economics etc., but rather that these subjective constructions preclude any possibility of clear moral guidance—just because they are subjective does not make them any less 'real'. Entire value systems are, as postmodernism contends, subjective creations. It is the very perception of value that creates value. Beyond the bonds of experience, value does not, nor ever has existed; when we speak of value and we speak of an individuals' perception, we are speaking of one and the same thing. However, once it is created, it is very real. In that they ultimately create the experience of suffering or the lack of it, morality is thus reified. That is, the parameters are created through a wholly subjective process, but once created, we live and die within these very parameters. The postmodern argument fails to recognize this truth, and it is precisely this truth that no amount of postmodern relativism can undermine.

How this is, and is not Utilitarianism

This might be understood as Utilitarianism, or perhaps even a refined version of hedonism. To a certain extent this is true. The basic goal of utilitarianism is to offer a means with which to arrive at somehow valid normative propositions regarding what is '"just" by positing the principle of maximizing individuals' experience of happiness as a way to gauge what is right.[25] Similarly, we are here positing 'happiness' as having intrinsic value. However, although similar, there is a slight difference: the emphasis here is *not on maximizing utility, but on finding a stable under footing of value on which to stand at all.* We can be said to be taking from utilitarianism only what is necessary to establish firm ground upon which to plant our footing upon the shifting sands of postmodern relativism. Issues of maximizing utility for the greatest good are purposively not brought into the discussion. The difference is: subjective reaction is not a tool with which to gauge the moral nature of an act, rather, *it is the moral nature of an act*—it is value. The point being made here is that subjective reaction is the very creation, or 'reification' of value. There is simply no value outside of this phenomenon, regardless of whatever convoluted expression it assumes. Value does not exist in a vacuum; it is an interpretive process.

Bentham once famously decried the notion of natural law as "nonsense upon stilts."[26] Let us now carry it further: the notion of objective value at all, is nonsense upon even higher stilts. Value is no more than an individual's subjective interpretation of events; an interpretation that can be enlarged to subsume entire cultures that have formed consensus around it. Thus, subjective reaction is not so much a mechanism through which we may quantify the moral nature of an act, rather, it is the very creation of value; value does not, nor ever has existed outside of this subjective process—as postmodernism suggests, it is solely a human construction. But, nevertheless, it is here in the core of this process of construction, that we can discover a degree of constancy.

CONCLUSION

Our reasoning here accepts full throttle the inevitable conclusions to which postmodern thought leads us: value is the machinations of culture and subjective reaction. But at the end of the day, the measure of certainty implicit in these very reactions provides stability within this moral turmoil. Bartley's reaction to unwashed grapes constructs the possibility of value, and brings it into existence where otherwise it simply would not be present. As Bartley's reaction is what allows the possibility of value, we can turn to the very reaction for moral guidance. To bemoan the fact that value constructs are subjective is rather odd, if not irrelevant; it does not matter. We eventually come full circle. The reaction *is* value. Thus, once created, it is as real as anything, and is a point of stability that postmodern moral relativism cannot undercut. It does not matter what course we follow to stimulate those reactions. Subjective concoctions or not, they are real. And they are foundational principles.

The postmodern argument is a powerful one precisely because it reveals in unapologetic clarity the true magnitude of our ignorance. The subjective nature of our conceptions of the world are exposed for what they are. Nevertheless, this does not disenfranchise morality. On the contrary, in that the process of deconstruction sets our value systems in proper relief, the moral superstructure on which they are based becomes that much clearer, and thus reinvigorated. Our value systems are stripped of all claims to objective authority, but yet the end result remains the same—it makes no difference. There is right and wrong. Ultimately, all post modernism does is force us to set aside the exterior expressions of "justice," and instead root our legal conceptions at this more fundamental level.

Value structures as reflected in the law may shift and change over time. As with all value systems, codified systems of law, and the principles they establish such as nuisance, trespass, and negligence, are highly determined by the particular cultural context from which they arise. However, it is in the intrinsically negative quality of suffering that we find firm footing on which to distinguish right from wrong—here we have a piece of 'reality' on to which we can firmly clutch. It is here that the laws we formulate cease to be arbitrary fabrications and become rooted in fixed moral truth. It is a simple and familiar formula: the generation of suffering is inherently bad; conversely, the cessation of human suffering is good. It is logistically difficult to quantify, but is endowed with a quality of reality, of universal truth, more than capable of withstanding the nihilistic blows of moral relativism engendered by postmodern thought. The basis of law has credence only in so far as it conforms to this principle, and no more.

Notes

1. "Restoration to the original position." *Oxford Dictionary of Law*, 464 (6th ed. 2006).

2. As one justice opined, there is indeed "a jungle of separate, broadly based jurisdictions all over the world." Lord Goff in Airbus Industri GIE v Patel 1 AC 199 (1999).

3. *See* Siman Deakin, Anguis Johnston & Basil Markesinis, *Markesiinis and Deakin's Tort Law*, 113 (6th ed. 2008), writing on negligence in particular ("Its expansion, in particular in the course of the twentieth

century, reflects the pressures that the rise of an industrial and urban society have brought to bear upon the traditional categories of legal redress for interference and protected interests. The growth and increasing sophistication of insurance have also contributed to this expansion. A doctrinal examination of negligence must not lose sight of this wider social and economic context within which the tort has developed, which is reflected in fluidity of the central legal concepts and the courts' ever-increasing recourse to 'policy' as an explanation of their decisions.") (footnotes omitted).

4. The fact that most people find the possibility that our beliefs are not grounded upon any objectively valid criteria frightening, perhaps points to the very motivation for believing in the conventions we do. That is, there is a deep human need to affix certain moral truths to ours systems of value as it provides a degree of emotional certainty that we are indeed correct in our beliefs, and our beliefs are not simply subjective concoctions, but rather are out there, existing as objective moral truths. In a sense, our reaction to the argument of postmodernism goes far in explaining why we believe there is objective truth in the first place, i.e. we simply need to. To pose the question differently, do we need to believe in the value systems we do because they are true, or do we believe them to be true because we need to? Perhaps, there is a greater emotional compulsion lurking behind our beliefs than we are willing to acknowledge. A good example of this is religious belief. The vast majority of individuals who boast deeply held religious beliefs, subscribe to the very religion in which they were raised to believe. It is remarkable how this fact does not cause intelligent people to question at least the motivation behind their religious convictions.

5. The Danish Penal Code 1995, s. 222 (1) states: "Any person who has sexual intercourse with any child under the age of 15 shall be liable to imprisonment for any term not exceeding 6 years."; *See also* Interpol, Legislation Of Interpol Member States On Sexual Offences Against Children (2009), *http://www.interpol.int/public/Children/SexualAbuse/NationalLaws/csaDenmark.asp* ("Age of consent for sexual activity: When a person is fifteen (15) years old s/he can consent to sexual intercourse").

6. For an informative listing of abolitionist states, see Hugo Adam Bedau, *The Death Penalty in America: Current Controversies,* 78-83 (1997).

7. Canadian Criminal Code 1985, s. 21(1) *(a)*.

8. The Separation Thesis essentially posits the idea that there is "a conceptual separation between law and morality, that is, between what the law is, and what the law ought to be . . . Once again, the

Separation Thesis, properly understood, pertains only to the conditions of legal validity. It asserts that the conditions of legal validity do not depend on the moral content of the norms in question. What the law is cannot depend on what it ought to be in the relevant circumstances. Many contemporary legal Positivists would not subscribe to this formulation of the Separation Thesis. A contemporary school of thought, called Inclusive Legal Positivism, endorses the Social Thesis, namely, that the basic conditions of legal validity derive from social facts, such as social rules or conventions which happen to prevail in a given community. But, Inclusive Legal Positivists maintain, legal validity is sometimes a matter of the moral content of the norms, depending on the particular conventions that happen to prevail in any given community. Those social conventions on the basis of which we identify the law may, but need not, contain reference to moral content as a condition of legality." *See* Andrei Marmor, Stanford Encyclopedia Of Philosophy, The Nature Of Law (2001), *http://plato.stanford.edu/entries/lawphil-nature/. See also,* Mark C. Murphy, *Natural Law in Jurisprudence and Politics,* 20-26 (2006).

9. *See* Marmor, *op. cit.* ("Legal Positivism can accept the claim that law is, by its very nature or its essential functions in society, something good that deserves our moral appreciation. Nor is Legal Positivism forced to deny the plausible claim that wherever law exists, it would have to have a great many prescriptions which coincide with morality. There is probably a considerable overlap, and perhaps necessarily so, between the actual content of law and morality.").

10. Indeed, the Law and Economics approach to legal study which flourished in the latter part of the twentieth century, might be conceptualised at yet another attempt to ground law in some underlying rationale, this being the idea of economic efficiency, or the rationale of utility as borrowed from the discipline of economics. The rationale is certainly distinct from, for instance, natural law thinking, but they are in a sense similar in that the approach is pinned to an underlying explanatory justification of sorts.

11. In the social norm literature see, e.g., Robert C. Ellickson, *The Evolution of Social Norms: A Perspective from the Legal Academy* (Yale Law School, Program for Studies in Law, Economics and Public Policy, Working Paper No. 230, 1999); Robert C. Ellickson, "The Aim of Order Without Law", 97 *Journal of Institutional and Theoretical Economics,* 150 (1994); Robert Cooter, "Expressive Law and Economics", 27 *Journal of Legal Studies,* 585 (1998); Richard H. McAdams, *The Origin, Development, and Regulation of Norms,* 96 *MICHIGAN LAW REVIEW* 338 (1997); Mark J. Roe, *Chaos and Evolution in Law and Economics,* 109 *HARVARD LAW REVIEW* 641 (1996); Cass R. Sunstein, *Social Norms and Social Roles,* 96

COLUMBIA LAW REVIEW 903 (1996); Eric Posner, *Law and Social Norms* (2000); Edna Ullman-Margalit, *The Emergence of Norms, (1978).*

12. *See* Reza Banakar & Max Travers, *An Introduction to Law and Social Theory,* 119 (2002).

13. *See generally,* Roberto Mangabeira Unger, *The Critical Legal Studies Movement* HARV. LAW REV. 561-675 (1983).

14. Gary Saalman, *Postmodernism and You: Law* (1996), *http://www.xenos.org/ministries/crossroads/dotlaw.htm*

15. *Id.*

16. Mark Kelman, *A Guide to Critical Legal Studies,* 14 (1987).

17. *Id.* at 70.

18. *Id.* at 14.

19. M. Foucault, *The History of Sexuality,* VOLUME I: An Introduction, 144 (1978).

20. "The views that nothing exists outside one's own mind, or that nothing such can be known to exist, are called Solipsism (literally, 'only-oneself-ism') Alan Robert Lacey, *Dictionary of Philosophy,* 305 (3rd ed. 1996).

21. Assuming no greater good could come of it.

22. Here, and throughout the remainder of the paper, the term 'suffering' is used for lack of a better word. However, what is meant here by "suffering" is any experience of that which we define as negative. This may not necessarily be as profound an experience as the word suffering implies. Indeed it may range from the mildest feeling of agitation, or discomfort, to the deepest depths of human anguish.

23. Some might argue that human suffering is useful and has a function in life, in that it is conducive to great art, or human progress, but this is just semantics. What these advocates of suffering are really saying is that great art or human progress is worth the suffering. However, something can only be 'worth it' if, in some way, it is a short-term sacrifice for a greater good. And what is 'good' but ultimately reducing suffering. There is no way around this.

24. Kant though, and many other philosophers who view conforms to a Deontological ethics, would adamantly disagree. Kant for one places emphasis on the act itself, and not merely the consequences of the act, famously arguing that it would be even wrong to lie to a murderer asking the whereabouts of a potential victim. *See* C. Korsgaard, "Kant on Dealing With Evil" in James P. Sterba, *Ethics : The Big Questions* (1998).

25. *See* Walter Sinnott-Armstrong, Stanford Encyclopedia Of Philosophy, Consequentialism (2003), *http://plato.stanford.edu/entries/consequentialism/* ("The paradigm case of consequentialism is utilitarianism, whose classic proponents were Jeremy Bentham (1789), John Stuart Mill (1861), and Henry Sidgwick (1907). . . . Classic Utilitarians held hedonistic act consequentialism. *Act consequentialism* is the claim that an act is morally right if and only if that act maximizes the good, that is, if and only if the total amount of good for all minus the total amount of bad for all is greater than this net amount for any incompatible act available to the agent on that occasion. *Hedonism* then claims that pleasure is the only intrinsic good and that pain is the only intrinsic bad. Together these claims imply that an act is morally right if and only if that act causes "the greatest happiness for the greatest number," as the common slogan says.") (footnotes omitted).

26. Jeremy Bentham, "Anarchical Fallacies; Being An Examination of the Declarations of Rights Issued During the French Revolution" in John Bowring, *The works of Jeremy Bentham,* 501 (1843).

Formalism or Pragmatism: Habeas Corpus Legal Philosophy in the Union and Confederate Governments of Civil War America

DAVID PEARLMAN*

INTRODUCTION - THE RELEVANCE OF HABEAS CORPUS IN POST-9/11 AMERICA

In the aftermath of the attacks on September 11, 2001, the Bush administration authorized the indefinite detentions of several hundred individuals, some of them American citizens. The decision facilitated police work by making it easier to capture suspected terrorists and prevent them from carrying out alleged conspiracies. The detainees were not charged with crimes nor allowed to see lawyers. Some detainees could not even plead their case in court.

An exigency as great as national security outweighed the interests of the individual, argued President Bush. He explained that the indefinite internment of civilians, or enemy combatants as they are often termed, proves necessary when the country's very existence may be at risk. This was not a time for legal technicality or political fastidiousness. As the old refrain goes, desperate times call for desperate measures, and the months following the crippling terrorist attacks of September 11, 2001, certainly qualified as a desperate time.

---

*...

Recognizing that exigent circumstances may require the compromising of civil liberties, our founding fathers, in Article 1, Section 9, Clause 2 of the Constitution, granted authority to suspend the writ of habeas corpus, a writ that requires that a detainee be brought to a civilian court for determination of whether he is lawfully imprisoned. The clause reads: "The privileges of the writ of habeas corpus shall not be suspended, unless when, in cases of rebellion or invasion, the public safety may require it." President Bush's decision to not pursue a formal suspension on the writ of habeas corpus, in part, led to the civil liberties debate that remains strong today. Short of death and torture, there can be no greater infringement on personal liberty than to sit in a cell indefinitely with no right to challenge your imprisonment.

It would be difficult to contest the indefinite detainments of civilians on legal grounds if the Bush administration, in conjunction with Congress, had formally suspended the writ of habeas corpus for a specified period of time. America had been invaded and many feared future waves of attack. Why didn't President Bush opt to suspend the writ?

A critical analysis and survey of the habeas corpus debate in Lincoln's America and the Confederate South answers this question. In contrasting the primarily legal pragmatist approach of the Lincoln administration to the mostly legal formalist approach of the Confederate South, we learn that one's philosophical view on the law (and not just the law itself) profoundly affects policy-making in a time of crisis. By analyzing the competing legal approaches of pragmatism and formalism within the framework of the Civil War, we learn the pros and cons of each method. We discover the tendency of executive leaders to sometimes combine elements from each approach (as both the North and South did) when attempting to defend a particular legal position. Knowing how legal pragmatism and legal formalism shaped the outcome of the Civil War tells us how the two philosophies might shape the outcome of our current war. We learn that when a nation finds itself divided and in conflict, a legal pragmatist interpretation of civil rights spurs victory while a formalist view ensures defeat.

HABEAS CORPUS IN LINCOLN'S AMERICA

Weeks into President Abraham Lincoln's first term in office, the bloodiest war in American history broke out in South Carolina. Southern states seceded from the Union and became a part of a new country called the Confederate States of America. Border states, through painstaking political bargaining, remained a part of the United States, although often in name only. Confederate sympathizers living in the border states openly sabotaged the American war effort. Baltimore, in particular, developed into a Northern haven for Confederate disorder.[1]

Under the Baltimore police chief, a group of Confederate loyalists destroyed railroad tracks running from the North into Baltimore. The demolition interrupted normal troop movements, thereby necessitating an alternative travel route. Instead of simply riding the trains into Washington, the soldiers now had to travel by sea, a process which took a considerable amount of time and effort. Concerned about the delays in troop deployment and the difficulty of sending supplies by boat[2], President Lincoln became the first president in decades to suspend the writ of habeas corpus:

> Order for President Lincoln to General Winfield Scott on April 27, 1861: To the Commanding General, Army of the United States:
>
> You are engaged in suppressing an insurrection against the laws of the United States. If at any point on or in the vicinity of any military line which is now or which shall be used between the city of Philadelphia and the city of Washington you find resistance which renders it necessary to suspend the writ of habeas corpus for the public safety, you personally, or through the officer in command at the point at which resistance occurs, are authorized to suspend the writ.
>
> Abraham Lincoln.[3]

President Lincoln's delegation of a power he may not have constitutionally held (suspension of the writ of habeas corpus without Congressional approval) first exploded into legal controversy with the arrest of John Merryman, one of the suspected criminal actors in the destruction of the Baltimore railroad line.[4] Chief Justice Roger Taney granted a writ of habeas corpus and ordered the Lincoln government to show cause in the detention of Merryman. A representative from Fort McHenry, which held Merryman, informed the Chief Justice that the writ of habeas corpus had been suspended. Refusing to recognize the suspension, Taney ordered the arrest of the commander of Fort McHenry. When the marshals arrived to arrest him, the commander simply remained inside the fort and did not permit them to enter. Undoubtedly infuriated, the Chief Justice then ruled in Ex parte Merryman that only Congress may suspend the writ of habeas corpus and that the government therefore had no right to indefinitely keep Merryman imprisoned.[5] President Lincoln refused to comply with the order, explaining his decision to a special session of Congress by invoking an argument that we often hear today. What good is punctilious adherence to a seemingly necessary law if, in the process of its exercise, we breed lawlessness and lose the country that created that law? In Lincoln's own words:

> ...the legality and propriety of what has been done...are questioned, and the attention of the country has been called to the proposition that one who has sworn to "take care that the laws be faithfully executed" should not himself violate them.... Must I have followed [the laws] to finally fail of execution, even had it been perfectly clear that by the use of the means necessary to their execution some single law, made in such extreme tenderness of the citizen's liberty, that practically it relieves more of the guilty than the innocent, should, to a very limited extent, be violated? To state the question more directly, are all the laws but one to go unexecuted, and the Government itself go to pieces, lest that one be violated?...would not the official oath be broken if the government should be overthrown, when it was believed that disregarding the single law would tend to preserve it?[6]

While President Lincoln's words could be interpreted as an admission to violating the law for, in his view, the greater good of preserving the nation, he tried to position himself as being on the correct side of the law. He viewed the Constitution as an adaptive framework colored by present day realities. He looked at the situation on the ground, made conclusions about what would be necessary to improve that situation, and then tried to justify his actions by fitting those conclusions within the guidelines of the Constitution. An imperfect fit meant only that the human experience had changed enough to alter interpretation of the Constitution. This common sense approach to the law and the acknowledgement that the Constitution cannot be interpreted in isolation from present day events allowed Lincoln to manipulate constitutional language creatively and conveniently in a way that would support his endeavors. Lincoln's position on the writ of habeas corpus underscored this use of legal pragmatism. He argued that the provision "the privilege of the writ of habeas corpus shall not be suspended, unless when, in cases of rebellion or invasion, the public safety may require it," certainly authorized suspending the writ in cases of rebellion or invasion. Since there was a Civil War taking place on American soil, a clear example of rebellion, Lincoln concluded that the habeas corpus provision applied. Furthermore, with the United States possibly collapsing, and violence and mayhem rampant throughout much of the nation, the public safety most certainly required it. As for who may exercise the authority to suspend the writ of habeas corpus, Lincoln referred to the silence of the Constitution itself as evidence of his authority in this area. He also highlighted the impracticality of waiting for Congress to convene, noting that emergencies may require immediate action. How could the framers have intended for the executive to remain inactive when the executive is best equipped to handle an exigent circumstance?[7] President Lincoln then deferred to his Attorney General, Edward Bates, for a more nuanced legal defense of the executive power to suspend the writ of habeas corpus. Not surprisingly, Lincoln's Attorney General also adopted a legal pragmatist perspective, although some would view it as legal recklessness.

Attorney General Bates' opinion to President Lincoln employed classic formalist techniques to reach pragmatic results. He began his advisory opinion by offering the conclusion that in times of danger and uprising, a president may disobey writs of habeas corpus and imprison "persons against whom there is probable cause for suspicion of...criminal complicity."[8] The Attorney General then worked backwards by explaining the system of checks and balances, and how each branch of government operated in its own co-equal sphere. He discussed the inherent conflict that came with a reciprocal approach to authority. He argued that the idea that a judicial decision bound the executive and that an executive decision bound the judiciary could not work unless both branches of government reached the same determination on that particular issue. Each branch of government served a particular set of constitutional functions and those constitutional functions could not be compromised (and effectively reversed) by edicts from another branch of government.[9] These arguments about the spheres of power, and the absolute nature of that power within each sphere, are familiar to formalist thought. Bates wrote:

> if the President be bound by the principles laid down by the judiciary, so also is the judiciary bound by the principles laid down by the President. And thus we shall have a theory of constitutional government flatly contradicting itself. Departments co-ordinate and coequal, and yet subordinate to each other! That cannot be. The several departments, though far from sovereign, are free and independent, in the exercise of the limited powers granted to them respectively by the Constitution.[10]

The Attorney General's contention that the inherent contradictions presented in a reciprocal theory of separation of powers necessitated independent operation of each branch is superficially persuasive at the theoretical level but unconvincing in actual practice. While in general an executive decision binding the judiciary and a judicial decision binding the executive would seem to be in conflict, the Attorney General should have heeded his own language about the importance of each co-equal branch fulfilling its constitutional obligations. An executive decision should be binding on the other branches of government if that decision falls within its constitutionally-mandated responsibilities. The same holds true for the legislature and its respective enactments and for the judiciary and its judgments. Reciprocity of enforcement is not a conflict so long as each branch acts within its constitutional authority. The problem lies in a branch trying reciprocally to enforce an unconstitutional decision.

The Attorney General mentioned the importance of each branch operating under its specific constitutional powers, but one wonders if he truly believed what he wrote. How else could he have reached the conclusion that reciprocity of enforcement was untenable? Separation of powers is also about checks and balances. Each branch has many constitutional opportunities for reversing the decision of another branch. The executive can veto a legislative bill. The legislature can override the presidential veto. The judiciary can invalidate a legislative or executive law. The legislature can perform an end-run around the judiciary by passing constitutional statutes or ratifying a new amendment. The executive can pick who serves in the judiciary. There exist all kinds of interdependent relationships between all three branches of government. Co-dependence, not independence, therefore drives American democracy. The problem is not reciprocity of enforcement, but determination of whether the moving and interceding branches act within their respective constitutional spheres when issuing or blocking a decision. Attorney General Bates grounded the debate in a discussion of branches acting independently because it advanced his theory of presidential supremacy. This may seem like a minor point given how the Attorney General then engaged in a proper discussion of the constitutional role of the Court but it emphasizes the philosophical, almost imperial, frame of mind behind President Lincoln's decision-making with regard to his contested legal authority to suspend the writ of habeas corpus. It also lends credence to the view that the Lincoln administration operated under a philosophy of legal pragmatism. The Attorney General's Hamiltonian common sense view of the executive's constitutional powers would provide President Lincoln with the authority to suspend the writ of habeas corpus and thereby wage war more effectively. Bates looked at the reality of the political circumstances and determined that the Constitution must be read in a manner consistent with strong presidential powers.

Attorney General Bates next evaluated the constitutional function of the judiciary. The judiciary's function, he wrote, was "to hear and determine cases, not to 'establish principles', nor 'settle questions', so as to conclude any person but the parties and privies to the cases adjudged."[11] This argument suggests that Bates devalued the use of judicial precedent, or at the very least opposed the creation of new precedent to "judge made law." Such a position is not surprising given the Attorney General's allegiance to the executive branch but it also happened to be an impractical one, given the existence of the common law for the last several centuries and the need for the law to be somewhat consistent and predictable. If by "establish principles" and "settle questions," the Attorney General referred to political issues as opposed to legal ones, then his point deserves merit. However, the context of his discussion involved presidential authority to suspend the writ of habeas corpus, a clearly legal determination, albeit with undeniable political ramifications.

Article 3, Section 2 of the Constitution defines judicial power as extending "to all cases in law and equity arising under this Constitution, the laws of the United States, and treaties made, and which shall be made, under their authority..." Section 2 then enumerates the types of cases and controversies that can be brought before the Court: controversies between states, cases affecting ambassadors and ministers, cases involving disputes between citizens of the states, citizens of foreign states, etc.[12] Nowhere in the enumeration, concluded Bates, did the judiciary have the right to impose rules or cast binding judgment on the other branches of government.[13]

The notion that the judiciary could not issue legal judgments against the executive or legislative branches appears to be clearly erroneous and therefore unlikely to represent his true position. The text of Article 3, Section 2, which Attorney General Bates himself quoted, says that judicial power "shall extend to *all* cases in law and equity arising under this Constitution..." Unless we conveniently view the executive branch as implicitly above the law, or unless we agree to respect sovereign immunity as absolute and unreviewable, it seems impossible to interpret "all cases in law and equity arising under this Constitution" as "all cases in law and equity arising under this Constitution except for those that arise as a result of disputes with the executive branch." Bates essentially proffered the editorialized definition as the correct interpretation. Legal history, common sense and the inclusive use of the word "all" seem to indicate otherwise. Secondly, the enumeration portion of Article 3, Section 2 explicitly mentions that the judiciary may hear "controversies to which the United States shall be a party." The 'United States' in this context refers to the government and, in practice, to an executive sub-department of it. Even if we assume for the sake of argument that Ex parte Merryman is not a case "in law and equity," it certainly ought to count as a controversy "to which the United States shall be a party." In Ex parte Merryman, the commander of Fort McHenry refused to comply with Chief Justice Taney's order to produce John Merryman in court. The Fort McHenry commander acted in the capacity of the federal government, on behalf of the United States.[14] This therefore involved a controversy "to which the United States shall be a party." Resolution of the specific Ex parte Merryman case thus created a precedent for other similar cases and indirectly established a set of legal principles by which to determine who could suspend the writ of habeas corpus, and under what conditions. Attorney General Bates' legal pragmatism was getting a little too convenient.

Attorney General Bates correctly pointed out that the judiciary could not establish direct explicit rules for the executive branch.[15] Justice Taney indeed may have overstepped his bounds in using one case to formally forbid all future presidents from suspending the writ of habeas corpus. On a practical level, however, the difference appears to be relatively insignificant. Justice Taney could have ruled that Lincoln could not suspend the writ of habeas corpus for John Merryman, and Taney could do the same for every similar case that emerged. Alternatively, President Lincoln could realize that the law was not on his side and that every instance in which he used the unconstitutional suspension of the writ of habeas corpus, he would be reversed, thereby rendering it an ineffective tool. Both methods would lead to the same ultimate result but the second one would be better for judicial economy purposes. If the president respected the precedent established by one case, other nearly identical cases would not emerge. The government would then save on both money and time.

The next argument raised by Attorney General Bates is that the executive had the power to detain people in order to ensure the presidential oath "that the laws be faithfully executed." This related back to President Lincoln's affirmative contention regarding the necessity to sidestep one law in order to uphold all the other laws. Bates pointed to a congressional statute from 1807 which allowed the president, at his own discretion, without court involvement, to use the military to oust intruders on public land.[16] He explained that this served as a precedent to allow presidents in wartime to arrest and indefinitely hold those suspected of criminal activity.[17]

The connection between the 1807 statute and the presidential suspension of habeas corpus appears to be a weak one. In Ex parte Merryman, Chief Justice Taney forbade executive suspension of the writ of habeas corpus; he did not proclaim that no one could ever suspend the writ. In the Act of 1807, conversely, Congress explicitly granted the president authority to arrest those who intruded upon publicly-owned land. President Jefferson did not act unilaterally; he sought permission from Congress and received it. If President Lincoln had sought permission from Congress to suspend the writ of habeas corpus and had been granted that power, then Justice Taney's decision in Ex parte Merryman presumably would have come out quite differently. The Court's issue was not the general constitutionality of suspending the writ of habeas corpus, but the constitutionality of having *the president* suspend the writ of habeas corpus. Bates made a specious claim here. He compared a congressionally-approved power delegated to the president to a power unilaterally taken by a president without congressional approval. He then somehow determined that the former therefore supported the legality of the latter. The Attorney General appeared to be forcing connections in an effort to justify his view of the Constitution.

In fairness to Attorney General Bates, there had been a tradition of courts deferring to presidents during times of crisis. A president was supposed to be able to exercise prerogative power with little interference from Congress and the Supreme Court.[18] Lincoln noted that "[A]s commander-in-chief of the army and navy, in time of war I suppose I have a right to take any measure which may best subdue the enemy."[19] Bates turned Lincoln's hesitance ("I *suppose* I have a right..." indicates uncertainty) into a full-fledged theory of presidential supremacy and authority to enact far-sweeping measures. He hinged this argument on the meaning of the presidential oath to "preserve, protect and defend" the Constitution, an oath unique to the president. Bates concluded that "putting down rebellion, insurrection, and all unlawful combinations to resist the general government" fell into these categories.[20] Given the plain English definitions of the words preserve, protect and defend, this seems like a reasonable conclusion that would at least have been within the spirit of the Constitution. Adherence to the spirit of the Constitution reveals a conspicuously legal pragmatist concern. If the president must ensure the survival of the Constitution, then he must defeat a rebellion that threatens to overturn the government, or else lose the Constitution that he was obligated to protect. How can there be victory if the Constitution becomes moot because of the disappearance of the country it was written for? This was the crux of the Attorney General's position. As Justice Jackson said in 1949, the Constitution is not a suicide pact.[21] The Constitution must be flexible enough to afford the executive substantial leeway in keeping the country together. Legal pragmatism becomes important here because war time differs from peace time. Context matters and cannot be ignored.

What kind of limits, if any, may be imposed on the president as he preserves the Constitution? Bates answered this question by explaining that the means for preservation, protection and defense of the Constitution could take on multiple forms. The Constitution does not prescribe the specific methods by which the president can carry out his oath because not all future changes and contingencies can be foretold. We know only that the president acts as commander in chief of the armed forces, and may therefore use the military to preserve, protect and defend the Constitution.[22] "If [the rebels] employ spies and emissaries...to forward rebellion" wrote Bates, the president "may find it both prudent and humane to arrest and imprison them."[23] Furthermore, explained the Attorney General, "the judiciary has no political powers...and therefore no court or judge can take cognizance of the political acts of the President, or undertake to revise and reverse his political decisions."[24] But as raised earlier in the context of reciprocal enforcement of one branch's decision on the actions of another, the suspension of the writ of habeas corpus did not belong solely to the political realm; it had serious legal and constitutional consequences that only the Court could authoritatively articulate. Attorney General Bates' nebulous description of open-ended presidential powers played loosely with legal pragmatism because pragmatism should not be misinterpreted as recklessness. Bates appeared to be minimizing the constitutional authority of other branches in a manner inconsistent to common sense and the real life controversies of his day. Whereas President Lincoln focused on legal pragmatism as an avenue towards supporting the presidential suspension of habeas corpus, Attorney General Bates used a mixture of pragmatism and simple convenience.

The most obvious example of Attorney General Bates' legal convenience can be found in his argument that the Supreme Court did not even know which writ the Constitution referenced in Article 1, Section 9, Clause 2. Bates discussed the history of the writ and traced its origins to England, where there existed many writs of habeas corpus, some quite different to the one President Lincoln thought he suspended.[25] Bates noted that even if the writ of habeas corpus written into the Constitution referred to habeas corpus ad subjiciendum (the writ demanding that the arrestor present the detainee and provide cause for his confinement)[26] there is no mention of who can suspend the writ, or of what "suspension" means. "Suspended – does that mean delayed, hung up for a time, or altogether denied?" asked Bates.[27] If the word "suspended" could be interpreted creatively and in line with the realities of contemporary circumstances, then President Lincoln could revise his presidential orders by doing something other than "suspension" of the writ of habeas corpus. For instance, he could have tried removing the Court's jurisdiction over habeas corpus petitions by passing a new statute through Congress that would limit lower court powers to issue writs. He would reach his same desired result; he would simply take an alternative route to get there. The Attorney General laid the groundwork for such an angle, it just seemed as though he would have preferred not to concede defeat to the judiciary's interpretation on the legislature's role as default suspender of the writ. Challenging the technical meaning of "suspended," and then comparing it to the president's allegedly contrasting actions, as opposed to focusing on who could do the actual suspending – regardless of what the word "suspended" means – weakened the president's standing. Victory on a technicality would have rung more hollowly than victory on the substantive merits. Arguing a strict technical point also ran against the Lincoln administration's otherwise legal pragmatist appeal to the public. In promoting presidential powers to suspend the writ of habeas corpus, the Lincoln administration would have been better off sticking to its theme that newer times and experiences ushered in newer interpretations of who could exercise constitutional power, and to what extent. By testing the validity of a few long-held legal understandings, such as which writ the "suspension of habeas corpus" referred to, and even the meaning of the word "suspension," the Attorney General delved into a formalist debate that he likely could not win. He came off as more desperate, and therefore less convincing, because he initially rejected rigid formalism at the macro level only to embrace it later in a narrower category. It would have been better to remain consistently pragmatist than to mix competing legal philosophies.

After mounting a series of formalist definitional challenges, Bates returned to legal pragmatism by taking a legal instrumentalist perspective to distinguish between judicial powers to issue a writ of habeas corpus and the individual's power to challenge his own detention.[28] While the instrumentalist challenge took on the form of a technical argument, it did so with a distinct societal goal of conducting a political balancing test. It therefore remains under the category of pragmatism. The Attorney General's decision to frame the seemingly technical discussion around abstract concepts of rights, privileges and good fortune supports this claim.

In launching the new argument about a distinction between judicial rights and individual privilege, the Attorney General first noted the precarious foundation of the courts and their right to issue writs. Congress could have repealed the Judiciary Act of 1789 and the Act of 1833 during wartime or at any time.[29] The constitutional provision on the suspension of habeas corpus predated both statutes, suggesting that the suspension clause applied to individual privilege, and not to a lower federal court's affirmative right when no such court even existed at the time of the Constitution's ratification.

The Judiciary Act of 1789 and the Act of 1833 granted the lower federal courts authority to issue writs of habeas corpus, and according to the Supreme Court's interpretation of the Constitution, only Congress could terminate that right – either temporarily during a time of exigency when the public safety required it or by repealing the Acts that granted the courts such authority in the first place. Thus a court's powers in this area existed only at the behest of Congress. Bates wrote that a court's primary concern in the habeas corpus matter must therefore be to protect its own powers to issue the writs and not the privileges of individuals to enjoy the benefits of these writs.[30] Bates implied here that while the Supreme Court might be correct about the legislature being the only branch that could suspend a lower court's power, the president could still suspend the individual's powers. Rights and privileges were not identical. The words should not be construed as synonymous, explained the Attorney General.[31] The courts enjoyed the right to issue writs of habeas corpus as a result of Congressional legislation. Individuals enjoyed the *privilege* of habeas corpus as a part of their American heritage. Article 1, Section 9, Clause 2 referred to "the *privileges* of the writ of habeas corpus," - not the rights. Because the president was not suspending rights enjoyed by the courts, nothing constitutionally stopped him from suspending the privileges enjoyed by individuals as a result of the writs. Lower courts still might be able to issue writs but the president had no duty to obey them. He could suspend the benefits ("the privileges") of the writ if he determines that the public safety required it.

In effect, an executive suspension of individual privilege led to the same result as a suspension of court authority to issue the writ. The suspension of the privilege canceled out judicial authority without actually removing or "suspending" any affirmative right. If the president could ignore the Court's reaffirmation of writs requiring the production of evidence against an incarcerated individual, then the Court would eventually stop issuing such writs because they would be rendered useless.

In Ex parte Merryman, Chief Justice Taney responded to President Lincoln and Attorney General Bates' claims about the constitutionality of the habeas corpus provision. Unlike the President and his Attorney General, Taney phrased his answer in a framework of legal formalism. Viewing the law as a matter of logic and science, he looked at the structure and precise language of the Constitution to reach the conclusion that the president could not suspend the writ of habeas corpus. He also used settled court precedent to make this determination.[32]

Ex parte Merryman involved the aforementioned case of John Merryman, an accused Confederate conspirator who allegedly dynamited a Baltimore railroad track. Justice Taney, undoubtedly in an effort to portray his test case in the most positive light, depicted Merryman as a peaceful family man unjustly roused from his bed during the dark early morning hours and sent into confinement at a military outpost for alleged crimes unsupportable by the factual evidence.[33] Because, as Taney mentioned, the Constitution forbade the president from suspending the writ of habeas corpus, or allowing inferior officers of the executive branch to do the same, Justice Taney, as authorized by the fourteenth section of the Judiciary Act of 1789, issued a writ of habeas corpus to inquire as to the specific reasons for Merryman's imprisonment.[34] Taney knew only that Merryman was arrested for treason and rebellion, and that no lists of witnesses or a summary of specific allegations were provided.[35]

The Chief Justice's first explanation as to why the president could not suspend the writ of habeas corpus involved prior precedent. As with most legal formalists, Chief Justice Taney respected tradition and looked to the past when trying to resolve a controversy in the present. In this case, he compared President Lincoln's situation to the Jeffersonian era when President Jefferson wanted to end the Aaron Burr conspiracy. President Jefferson never claimed he could suspend the writ of habeas corpus on his own. Rather, he consulted Congress. Jefferson's respect for the legislature's constitutional role in suspending the writ indicated an early presidential understanding of the Constitution in line with Taney's.[36] If President Jefferson - one of the nation's founders – could see that only Congress had the authority to suspend the writ of habeas corpus, why couldn't President Lincoln see the same? The answer to this question gets back to the underlying theme of pragmatism versus formalism. President Jefferson did not have to deal with a Civil War. His desire to suspend the writ of habeas corpus did not rise to the same level of necessity as President Lincoln's.

The Chief Justice did not seem to contemplate the problem of gradation or scale. In his formalist view, what was applicable for Jefferson should be equally as applicable for Lincoln, or any other president. It was the same Constitution, and the Constitution did not change on the basis of external circumstances. Considerations that had applied to a vice-president's act of treason in a law-enforcement setting should apply equally to a popular insurrection that threatened the nation's survival. Taney succinctly explained that the habeas corpus clause appeared in the first article of the Constitution – an article that created the legislative branch without "the slightest reference to the executive department."[37] The first article began by mentioning "that all legislative powers therein granted shall be vested in a Congress of the United States, which shall consist of a Senate and House of Representatives." After explaining the form of election, the first article enumerated the legislative powers, including Section 9, Clause 2 which authorized suspension of the writ of habeas corpus.[38] Taney's clear and concise structural explanation served as the foundation for his next line of attack against the more haphazard pragmatist approach of Lincoln and Bates.

Continuing on the formalist structure argument, the Chief Justice looked at the specific placement of the privilege of the writ of habeas corpus clause. The clause not only appears under Article 1 (the legislative branch), it appears at the beginning of the list of Congress' prohibited powers. In Taney's own lucid words:

> The great importance which the framers of the Constitution attached to the privilege of the writ of habeas corpus, to protect the liberty of the citizen, is proved by the fact, that its suspension, except in cases of invasion or rebellion, is first in the list of prohibited powers; and even in these cases the power is denied, and its exercise prohibited, unless the public safety shall require it.[39]

Using legal logic, another reliable indication of formalism, the Chief Justice explained that if the president were meant to exercise power "over the liberty of the citizen," the privilege of the writ of habeas corpus provision would have been written, in plain language, into the second article of the Constitution which described the powers of the executive branch.[40] Instead, "there is not a word in it [the second article] that can furnish the slightest ground to justify the exercise of the power."[41] While the Chief Justice appeared to be using a degree of hyperbole (the president certainly has some degree of constitutional authority over something as general as "liberty of the citizen,") he did so in order to draw attention to the lack of formalist legal authority behind the Lincoln administration's legal assertions. If the Chief Justice could assert that Lincoln's actions did not contain even a scintilla of legal support, then perhaps the president could be persuaded to pursue his war-time endeavors through their proper constitutional channels - something the Republican president likely could have done earlier, given the realities of an overwhelmingly Republican Congress[42] willing to grant retroactive approvals of Lincoln's suspensions of the writ.[43]

There had even been legal support for Congressional retroactive approval. Justice James Wayne wrote that "Congress has constitutional power to legalize and confirm executive acts, proclamations, and orders done for the public good, although they were not, when done, authorized by any existing laws."[44] In other words, it was legally acceptable (according to Wayne) that Lincoln acted alone in suspending the writ of habeas corpus, so long as Congress eventually approved the suspension; if Congress would not do so, then that's all that was legally required. But why not go to Congress to begin with? One reason had to do with a simple matter of timing. Congress was not in session during the first suspension of habeas corpus. In addition, Lincoln did not want Congress meddling with his management style during the early stages of the Civil War.[45] For example, Delaware Senator James Bayard, a Democrat, claimed that Lincoln was "declaring himself a Dictator,"[46] while Ohio Senator John Sherman, a Republican, in agreement with Lincoln's overall approach, felt that Lincoln's unilateral suspension of the writ of habeas corpus was not "strictly legal, and in consonance with the provisions of the Constitution."[47] If Lincoln could avoid the nuisance of explaining himself to his critics at every step of the way, he could focus on more pressing matters. Carving out Hamiltonian rights for the presidency was thus essential for the efficiency of Lincoln's office. That's why he showed reluctance to immediately approach Congress. He simply did not deem it necessary or worth the trouble.

The suspension of habeas corpus in Baltimore was not the only time that President Lincoln would suspend the writ. Justice Taney undoubtedly understood the importance of trying to clamp down early on Lincoln's self-proclaimed legal authority before he exercised it broadly without Congressional support.

To limit Lincoln's authority, Taney reminded him of what the Constitution permitted for a president with regard to military powers and the arrests of individuals without due process of law. The Chief Justice, while recognizing many of the president's Article 1 powers, pointed out limitations on his military powers including state appointment of officers. In Taney's view, the constitutional check against the appointment of state officers served "as a security against the use of military power for purposes dangerous to the liberties of the people, or the rights of the states..."[48] Jumping to the Fifth Amendment, the Chief Justice explained that the due process clause expressly prohibited the federal government (the president included) from depriving someone of life, liberty or property.[49] The indefinite detention of suspected Confederate spies therefore violated the due process clause of the Constitution.

The president's only role in a citizen's liberty revolved around his Article 2, Section 3 obligation to "take care that the laws shall be faithfully executed." Contrary to Attorney Bates' contention, Taney ruled that the president could not execute these laws himself or through subordinating officers, independently of the other branches of government. The president's role was "to take care that they be faithfully carried into execution, as they are expounded and adjudged by the coordinate branch of the government to which that duty is assigned by the Constitution."[50] In other words, the president served an enforcement capacity. It was his job to make sure that the legislature's laws went into effect and that the judiciary's decrees became implemented. The president himself should not make the laws or hand down the judgments. When dealing with a judicial decision, "... he acts in subordination to judicial authority, assisting it to execute its process and enforce its judgments."[51]

Lest President Lincoln attempt to suspend the writ of habeas corpus by directly pressuring Congress to do so, Chief Justice Taney once again went to precedent in order to dismiss the notion that Lincoln could play any role in Congress' decision. Attorney General Bates had argued that the suspension of the writ of habeas corpus amounted to a political decision and that the executive branch, much like the legislature, served a political function. Therefore, argued Bates, the president should be able to determine when an exigency required the suspension of the writ. The Chief Justice rejected this premise by invoking Justice Story's expression of deference to Congress in his *Commentaries on the Constitution*:

> Hitherto no suspension of the writ has ever been authorized by Congress since the establishment of the constitution. It would seem, as the power is given to congress to suspend the writ of habeas corpus in cases of rebellion or invasion that the right to judge whether the exigency had arisen must exclusively belong to that body.[52]

Chief Justice Taney's last major argument revolved around the Tenth Amendment: "the powers not delegated to the United States by the constitution, nor prohibited by it to the states, are reserved to the states, respectively, or to the people." The Constitution enumerated both affirmative powers and prohibitive ones. Any powers not delegated within the Constitution belonged to the states or the people. A president could not assert something that did not expressly fall within his Article 2 powers.[53]

As the Civil War waged on, President Lincoln continued to ignore Chief Justice Taney and suspended the writ of habeas corpus numerous times. One of these more famous instances included the 1862 suspension of the writ in order to aid in the arrest of draft dodgers and those who abetted them or conspired against the United States more generally. The seemingly all-inclusive proclamation essentially allowed Lincoln to arrest anyone and keep that person locked up until the end of the War. Spurred by an increase in public uneasiness with the concept of indefinite detentions, President Lincoln took aim at the courts, branding them as ineffective during a time of war.[54] In doing so, he embraced a legal pragmatist interpretation of the Constitution:

> Presidential Proclamation Suspending the Writ of Habeas Corpus Because of Resistance to the Draft:
>
> Whereas it has become necessary to call into service not only volunteers, but also portions of the militia of the States by draft, in order to suppress the insurrection existing in the United States, and disloyal persons are not adequately restrained by the ordinary processes of law from hindering this measure...be it ordered– first, that during the existing insurrection...all rebels and insurgents, their aiders and abettors within the United States, and all persons discouraging volunteer enlistments, resisting militia drafts, or guilty of any disloyal practice affording aid and comfort to rebels against the authority of the United States, shall be subject to martial law...second, that the writ of habeas corpus is suspended in respect to all persons arrested, or who are now, or hereafter during the rebellion shall be, imprisoned in any...place of confinement, by any military authority..."[55]

The phrase "disloyal persons are not adequately restrained by the ordinary processes of law" pointed towards Lincoln's embrace of legal pragmatism and its idea that other considerations had to play into the determination of how one proceeded during an unparalleled time. Rather than adhere to the strict logical formalism of Chief Justice Taney who looked at constitutional structure, plain language and prior precedent, President Lincoln worked from the vantage point of political reality. He knew that the court process would be too complicated for a Civil War that required prompt resolution to complex life-threatening situations. Relying on the traditional court system and all its formalist trappings would play into the hand of the Confederacy by allowing Southern sympathizers to roam the streets of the North and continue their conspiracies. Clearly, in Lincoln's view, the founding fathers erred by not foreseeing as a realistic possibility the dissolution of the nation they founded. If they could have known what would transpire, Lincoln probably thought, would they not adopt the same method and work to re-read the law in a manner consistent with the exigency of the times?

Chief Justice Taney's formalist perspective worked well for someone who did not have to answer to a terrified war-torn public or deal with draft-dodgers on and off the battlefield on a daily basis. But what should a president do when he sees his country crumbling? If he adopted Chief Justice Taney's view, the United States would likely loses the war. It was always easier to imprison first and check for justice later. One can also understand why President Lincoln had preferred suspending the writ of habeas corpus on his own rather than embroiling himself in cumbersome Congressional debates where the inevitable partisan gridlock would have created inefficiency and generated unwanted publicity. Political reality affects the legal pragmatist perspective. Unlike structural arguments, which for the most part remain the same regardless of the times, legal pragmatism tends to be less predictable from one moment to the next. Many formalist jurists criticized legal pragmatism for this very reason. They believed that the law must be rooted in logic, tradition and predictability in order to avoid randomness and the chaos that comes with it. President Lincoln cleverly turned this around on the formalists by pointing out that judicial inflexibility brought chaos. If only the Court would have gotten with the times, the president would not have felt obligated to suspend the writ of habeas corpus and to take other seemingly drastic measures to ensure the public safety. By pointing out in the above suspension of the writ the inadequacy of the "current processes of law," Lincoln put the Court on the defensive. By going to the Congress a few months later and encouraging it to pass an act affirmatively granting the president retroactive authority to suspend the writ of habeas corpus (essentially whenever he saw fit)[56], the president possibly weakened the force of some of the Court's arguments about the need to let Congress decide whether to suspend the writ of habeas corpus. The lack of Congressional approval had always been the primary reason for the Court's legal opposition to the president's suspension of the writ. Now it could not use that argument anymore because Congress had been included in the decision. However, if by passing "An Act Relating to Habeas Corpus, And Regulating Judicial Proceedings In Certain Cases," Congress delegated its constitutional role of suspending the writ to the president, then the nature of the formalist versus pragmatist argument fundamentally would evolve into a discussion of whether one branch can delegate its powers to another. A formalist would argue that delegation of a Congressional power to another branch required a change in the Constitution via the amendment process. A statute could not invalidate or shift a constitutional responsibility. Thus, President Lincoln, even with congressional permission to suspend the writ of habeas corpus, acted unconstitutionally.

The one tangible benefit in passing the statute likely occurred in the realm of public opinion. Prior to the statute, concerned private citizens looked to Lincoln with skepticism. They figured that he was a despot acting unilaterally and without the will of the people. After the Habeas Corpus Act, these same people could have at least pointed towards congressional delegation of the suspension authority as tacit legislative approval of Lincoln's methods. For the average layperson with no legal training, it would have made no difference whether Congress authorized each suspension of the writ of habeas corpus or whether the president did so under a congressional statute granting him the discretion to suspend the writ of habeas corpus himself.

HABEAS CORPUS IN THE CONFEDERACY

Unlike President Lincoln and his officers who dealt swiftly with rebellion and insurrection by unilaterally suspending the writ of habeas corpus and capturing as many suspected Confederate operatives as possible, Confederate President Jefferson Davis's administration worked diligently to avoid any suspension of the writ of habeas corpus.[57] The Southern president made a concerted effort to prevent even the perception of the state trampling on the civil liberties of Union or Confederate citizens because he believed in the formalist rule of law and wished to distinguish his administration from that of the more brazen President Lincoln.[58] The Confederate States of America Constitution, almost a carbon copy of its Union counterpart, provided under its description of the legislative branch that "the privilege of the writ of habeas corpus shall not be suspended, unless when in cases of rebellion or invasion the public safety may require it." (Article 1, Section 9, Clause 3 instead of Article 1, Section 9, Clause 2.)[59] Despite the identical wording and near identical placement of the habeas provision in both the Union and Confederate constitutions, the Davis administration did not share Lincoln's view on presidential powers. In the spirit of Justice Taney's opinion in Ex parte Merryman (which did not apply to the Confederacy), Davis never attempted to suspend the writ of habeas corpus without specific approval from Congress.[60] Davis asserted that he would abide by the plain language of the Constitution that established his office.[61] The standard for an arrest in the South was thus much higher than the standard applied in the North. Military arrests could still be made under the theory that insurgents, by definition, repudiated their citizenship in the Confederacy and remained members of the United States.[62] As such, Confederate military officers regarded the insurgents as foreign aliens subject to prisoner of war status. President Davis used a U.S. Supreme Court case from 1830 as authority for his decision.[63] He based his positions on formalist legal reasoning: logic, structure, plain language and precedent.

Although thousands of arrests were made, many Confederate leaders worried about whether these arrests were justified. Confederate General John Winder, who like his Union counterpart at Fort McHenry, commanded a prison detention center, cooperated with the legal apparatus of his state. He also advocated on the behalf of his prisoners, recommending that they receive a fair opportunity to clear themselves. He asked the Confederate War Department to create a special commission to review each prisoner's detention, and the War Department granted the request.[64]

Confederate Secretary of War Judah Benjamin, a lawyer, also emphasized the importance of working within the law to respect the personal freedoms of the people.[65] He drew an implicit contrast to Lincoln's United States, a country that disrespected personal freedoms during times of exigency and whose president interpreted the law pragmatically, worrying more about the proverbial big picture than the small. In Benjamin's case, the concern was two-tiered. The fledgling Confederate Republic not only saw itself on a political quest to be recognized and respected as an independent united entity but also viewed itself as being in the midst of a philosophical struggle to maintain the core legal values that had made the ante-bellum United States a beacon of liberty. Consequently, almost no one spoke out in favor of legal pragmatism during the early years of the Confederate South. Whereas President Lincoln had favored legal pragmatism and spoke of the importance of sidestepping one law in order to keep the country together, Secretary Benjamin and most other Southern leaders took the opposite view, essentially arguing that if any law, particularly one as serious as habeas corpus relief, were to be ignored, then what good would the country be that had ignored it? The Confederate States of America would be no different than the United States. A major point of the war effort was to fight for the liberties that had been lost. How could a president, in good faith, circumvent liberty in order to preserve a new nation founded upon liberty? The Confederacy had no choice but to align itself with legal formalism. The conception of individual legal rights as a paramount virtue even in a time of war repeatedly emerged as a major Confederate theme. The new country took pride in its fair treatment of prisoners[66] during a period when it would have been far easier to simply imprison every rabble-rouser in sight. Secretary Benjamin described the process as follows:

> Prisoners held in jail are examined, and if guilty or believed to be guilty of treason or other crime against the State or Confederacy are handed over to the civil power, because ours is a Government of law, and it is our highest and proudest boast so to maintain it. Numerous prisoners have been thus transferred by this Department to the courts of justice. All others are released for our citizens cannot be held in jail on suspicion, and let us thank Providence that this exemption from violence to personal liberty is one of the...most precious fruits of the struggle in which we are engaged...Surely you would not have desired in the interest of your own liberty and that of those most dear to you that the violent hand of military power should have been laid on these men...[67]

After the initial phase of the Civil War ended on a losing note, the Confederate South found itself in desperate need of a more aggressive military track. Northern troops had converged on Fort

Monroe, near Tidewater, Virginia. Norfolk, Richmond (the capital) and Portsmouth were all under threat.[68] Thus on February 27, 1862, a secret session of Congress authorized the suspension of the writ of habeas corpus. The legislation was succinct:

> The Congress of the Confederate States of America do enact, That during the present invasion of the Confederate States, the President shall have power to suspend the privilege of the writ of habeas corpus in such cities, towns and military districts as shall, in his judgment, be in such danger of attack by the enemy as to require the declaration of martial law for their effective defense.[69]

In providing for declaration of martial law and recommending specific locations for the suspension of the writ of habeas corpus, and those locations only[70], Davis carried himself as someone whom his public could trust. He did not feel comfortable expanding the suspension of the writ over vast territories because he did not want to lose sight of what Secretary Benjamin and other civil liberty formalists of his day had promoted - a new nation that would respect the law, not treat it as an inconvenience to be dispensed with or could be manipulated easily by so-called pragmatism. Despite the president's self-restraint, many Confederate Congressmen grew uncomfortable with suspension of the writ. Representative John Baldwin of Virginia, a former colonel, offered a resolution to require the Committee on the Judiciary to investigate and define more narrowly martial law and imprisonments "for reasons of state."[71] He wanted to discover new ways for the Confederacy to control insurrections without suspending the writ of habeas corpus.[72] The move proved successful because a bill was passed to limit the suspension of the writ to "arrests made by authorities of the Confederate Government, or for offenses against the same."[73] Baldwin tried to restrict presidential powers even further by offering an amendment to a bill that would require the president to reveal before Congress each and every arrest that had been made resulting in an imprisonment. (This amendment ultimately failed).[74] If President Davis was going to continue receiving Congressional support for each suspension of the writ of habeas corpus, Baldwin at least wanted to know more about the people being confined. Fellow Confederate Congressman Henry Foote of Tennessee, also concerned about the spate of suspensions of the writ of habeas corpus (quite minor in comparison to the arrests that took place in the North), sought passage of a bill that would assemble a special committee to look into civil liberties abuses among detainees.[75] The goal of the proposed committee would be to report any intentional constitutional violations being made under military authority.[76] This concern for incarcerated individuals even became an issue during times when the writ was not suspended. In an advisory letter from Confederate Attorney General Thomas Hill Watts to President Jefferson Davis, dated August of 1863, the Attorney General discussed the need to be far more specific when responding to a writ of habeas corpus. He also touched upon the basic constitutional rights of the detainee:

> ...the return of Genl. Buckner to the writ is not sufficient: He should have stated the facts, and not his conclusions from the facts. He should have shown under what specific charge Abe Tipton was held, and who he was, and by what authority specially he held him in custody. He was bound also, in my judgment, to produce the body of Abe Tipton before the judge. The prisoner could not otherwise enjoy his full constitutional privileges. He has the right to be heard by himself and with counsel. He must be present to enjoy his right to contest the return.[77]

As one can see from the above examples, the formalist concern for the rule of law even during the height of the Civil War affected multiple branches of government in the Confederate South. The president exercised self-restraint, the Attorney General impressed upon the president the importance of constitutional privileges for those seeking to enjoy the benefits of habeas corpus, numerous legislators spoke up against suspension of the writ, and several more could not be mollified by anything short of strict Congressional oversight and limited extension of the suspension. Working within the constitutional framework became obligatory. The South did not want to win this war by reducing itself, in its view, to the North's legal pragmatist approach of doing whatever it took to win from a socio-political perspective, and then using hindsight to weave together a legal theory to justify it after the fact.

Concern for personal liberties reached a point bordering hysteria in 1864 when a desperate President Jefferson Davis found no other recourse but to temporarily dispense with the writ of habeas corpus and suspend it throughout the territory he controlled.[78] The Union army had effectively infiltrated much of the Confederate South and unless the rebels acted swiftly, visions for a country founded on legal formalism and strong civil liberties (slavery being an enormous exception) would never come to fruition. In an ironic, albeit not surprising twist of fate, legal formalism became one of the major adversaries of the Confederacy's survival unless President Davis could garner congressional support for his broad suspension of the writ. President Lincoln realized the practical problems with using ordinary civilian courts to deal with insurrection back during the opening months of the Civil War. President Davis had to acquiesce in that same practical realization. In a speech that would be reminiscent of one of Lincoln's many statements on the matter, Davis explained the suspension of the writ of habeas corpus as follows:

> ...a remedy plainly contemplated by the Constitution. All the powers of the Government, extraordinary as well as ordinary, are a sacred trust, to be faithfully executed whenever the public exigency may require...And a suspension of this writ when demanded by the public safety is as much a duty as to levy taxes for the support of the Government...It is idle to appeal against it to the history of the old Union. That history contains no parallel case. England, whose reverence for their great writ of right is at least as strong as our own, and the stability of whose institutions is the admiration of the world, has repeatedly, within the last hundred years, resorted to this remedy when only threatened with invasion. It may occasion some clamor but this will proceed chiefly from the men who have already too long been the active spirits of evil. Loyal citizens will not feel danger, and the disloyal must be made to fear it. The very existence of extraordinary powers often renders their exercise unnecessary. To temporize with disloyalty in the midst of war is but to quicken it to the growth of treason..."[79]

President Davis' assertions that the suspension of the writ of habeas corpus only affected disloyal persons is reminiscent of arguments we heard from the Bush administration following September 11th, 2001, and passage of the Patriot Act. President Davis tried to sell the people of the Confederacy on the idea that only the enemy would have something to hide. Why worry about the right to contest one's imprisonment if no crime is being committed? Rarely do fully innocent people get embroiled in a wrongful detention.

To his Confederate Congress, President Davis offered a typical Lincolnesque argument about the importance of fulfilling the executive obligation to protect the government by faithfully executing the Constitution and using its provisions as necessary.[80] Fortunately for Davis and the legal formalism his administration espoused, his arguments won. On February 11 of 1864, Congress approved its expansive Habeas Corpus Act.[81]

The preamble to the Act explained how the constitutional provisions covering the suspension of the writ remained solely in the control of Congress. It was critically important from a legal history perspective for the Confederate government to emphasize this point. By having Congress suspend the writ, as opposed to President Davis, there could be no obvious legal line of attack. The legislature performed its role as mandated by the Constitution and the president only served as an advisor, a well-informed leader who would keep the Congress abreast of developments regarding the public safety.[82] In letting Congress suspend the writ and affirmatively assert in written text its constitutional powers in that capacity, President Davis stayed true to legal formalism. This stood in stark contrast to President Lincoln, who at least during the earlier years of the War, forged his own path via legal pragmatism. The two presidents ended in the same place but arrived there by different legal philosophies.

Legal philosophy aside, the content of the Habeas Corpus Act remained controversial for a majority of southerners.[83] The Habeas Corpus Act covered thirteen categories of possible anti-Confederate infractions, including: espionage, treason, trading with the enemy, desertion, harboring deserters, inciting rebellion, injuring lines of communication and keeping unapproved munitions plants, etc.[84] Confederate officers could arrest and hold people indefinitely without needing to produce evidence beyond general suspicion.[85]

Although some influential Confederate leaders, including Howell Cobb, president of the Provisional Congress, and L.Q.C. Lamar, a Southern diplomat and future Supreme Court Justice, supported the measures of President Davis on both political and constitutional grounds, the majority of prominent Southern leaders opposed the Habeas Corpus Act. Some even deemed it unconstitutional.[86]

The Vice President of the Confederate States of America, Alexander Stephens, in a speech to the Georgia legislature in 1864, oddly went against his own president and railed against the Habeas Corpus Act on both political and constitutional grounds.[87] Like

President Lincoln, Stephens used legal pragmatism to arrive at his conclusion about the constitutionality of suspending habeas corpus. The difference is that Stephens used legal pragmatism to reach the opposite conclusion. In his view, there were no exigent circumstances. No good social outcome could be achieved by depriving people of any legal recourse to challenge their detentions.[88] Under that context, Stephens interpreted the Habeas Corpus Act as unconstitutional in spite of the Congressional approval it received. He explained that the power to suspend the writ comes by implication, not express delegation, and that an implication can never oppose a direct prohibition.[89]

"...The writ of habeas corpus shall not be suspended unless" implies that it can be suspended. However, if the Constitution meant for the writ to be suspended, then why not say so expressly? Direct express language must always supercede implication.[90] Furthermore, argued Stephens, there were conflicting express provisions in the Confederate Constitution that would cancel out the implied power to suspend the writ of habeas corpus. These included: (1) "the right of the people to be secure in their persons, houses, papers, and effects, against unreasonable searches and seizures...," (2) "no warrants shall issue but upon probable cause, supported by oath or affirmation, and particularly describing the place to be searched, and the persons or things to be seized," (3) "no person shall be deprived of life, liberty or property, without due process of law," and (4) "in all criminal prosecutions the accuser shall enjoy the right of a speedy and public trial by an impartial jury of the State or District where the crime shall have been committed; and to be informed of the nature and the cause of the accusation..."[91] In addition, said Stephens, the Executive's role did not include the arrests of civilians. A person cannot be held answerable for a crime "...unless on a presentiment or indictment of a grand jury, except in cases arising in the land or naval forces, or in the militia when in actual service time of war or public danger."[92] Notice the absence of a comma between "in actual service time of war" and "or public danger." This suggests that only military forces, either in their active military capacity or in a time of public danger were being discussed in this section. Therefore, explained Stephens, the Executive could not be delegated power to arrest non-military citizens. Only Congress could possibly do that and Congress could not give away its constitutional function to another branch.[93] To do so would be "to revive the odious practice of ordering political arrests...so long since renounced by our English ancestors, and the denial of the right of the constitutional judiciary to investigate such cases..."[94] The Confederate Congress cannot constitutionally permit unconstitutional arrests. When in doubt, argued Stephens, the state should err on the side of liberty and express statements. Why not allow the judiciary to perform its constitutional function?[95] To close out the section of his speech on the writ of habeas corpus, the Confederate Vice President made a populist appeal to the public, exclaiming that Congress "must maintain our liberties against encroachment and wipe this and all such stains from the statute book, or the Sun of Liberty will soon set in darkness and blood."[96] The use of poetic imagery bolsters the contention that Stephens relied upon theories of legal pragmatism. He allowed logic to follow his conclusion rather than let his conclusion follow logic.

Vice President Stephens' strong populist opposition to the suspension of the writ of habeas corpus led in part to the unwillingness of the Confederate Congress to extend suspension of the Habeas Corpus Act.[97] And so even though President Davis said that he was "indebted" to the suspensions "for the increased efficiency of the military preparations" and that "it would be perilous, if not calamitous, to discontinue the suspension,"[98] the Confederate Congress allowed the Act to expire without a renewal of the suspension.[99] Less than a year later, the Confederate Army surrendered to the Union and the Civil War came to an end. The short-lived Confederacy was repatriated into the United States.

CONCLUSION – THE DOWNFALL OF FORMALISM AND HOW IT AFFECTS PRESENT DAY DETENTIONS

One possible reason why President Bush opted not to work with Congress to suspend the writ of habeas corpus was because his administration learned two lessons from history. The experiences of the Civil War teach us that the legal philosophy that a president pursues during war time can help determine whether he emerges in victory or crawls into defeat. President Lincoln, adopting a line of thinking that would be familiar to the neo-conservatives of today, believed that a president must simply do whatever must be done in order to achieve a greater moral objective (in Lincoln's case, to defeat the institution of slavery and keep the nation together, in Bush's case, to defeat international terrorism and save the nation from a proliferation of domestic homicide attacks launched from abroad.) By choosing legal pragmatism, a philosophy that accommodated his policy goals, Lincoln won the Civil War. He knew what he had to do (in his mind) and so he analyzed the context of his times and allowed it to shape his legal arguments. From the framework of his plan, he cobbled together a legal theory of presidential power to suspend the writ of habeas corpus.

Jefferson Davis did the opposite. Like the early legal formalist of the U.S. Supreme Court, Chief Justice Taney, Davis did not want to copy the technically illegal actions of President Lincoln. Lincoln was viewed as a despot who would take away their property and their way of life, and the Confederacy wanted to project a more libertarian image. Thus Davis made quite sure to adhere to the letter of the law, even if it meant avoiding suspensions of the writ entirely for fear of not gaining Confederate congressional approval. When Davis finally suspended the writ, he did so only with the permission of Congress and an affirmation on its part that Congress would control the duration and extent of the suspension. When a divided Confederate Congress opted not to extend the suspension during the most critical stage of the Civil War, Davis allowed the suspension to expire. He did not defy his Supreme Court in the way that Lincoln openly defied Justice Taney. He did not create post hoc legal theories premised on exigency or silent powers. He dedicated himself to the tradition, logic and precedents of formalist law, and it led to his downfall. Vice President Stephens, whose opposition to suspending the writ of habeas corpus became the more popular view, used Lincoln's legal pragmatism and it worked. The conception of the law as something malleable and socially-based allowed both Lincoln and Stephens to champion their opposing theories with an overwhelming degree of success. Only the context-neutral positions of Taney and Davis failed, although Taney's decision proved influential as evinced by Lincoln's eventual change in tactics to get Congress to support a suspension of habeas corpus. President Bush also must recognize the importance of judicial precedent which explains, in part, why he has chosen not to travel down the exact same path as President Lincoln. The

Supreme Court has already ruled on executive authority to suspend the writ of habeas corpus, and as a legal pragmatist in the realm of military policy, Bush understands that a public already weary over the Patriot Act would not approve of a suspension of the writ of habeas corpus, even with Congressional approval. Thus it becomes easier to use that same legal pragmatism to forge a new path of constitutional theory about the expanding powers of the executive branch to detain individuals. Rather than pursue the habeas corpus route, it makes greater sense to label targeted suspects as "enemy combatants" and imprison them on foreign soil where American laws and protections arguably do not apply. Right or wrong, President Bush currently follows Lincoln's lead when it comes to using one's understanding of the times to create a legal theory that supports a desired political policy. And in that sense, the Civil War-era habeas corpus debate lives on through the prism of legal philosophy. It serves as a lesson to the leaders of today, and as a somber warning for the war-waging formalists of tomorrow.

Notes

1. Rehnquist, William. Civil Liberty and the Civil War. (Washington: The National Legal Center for the Public Interest, 1997.) 11.
2. *Id.* at 11-12.
3. Order from President Lincoln, April 27, 1861. Life and Works of Abraham Lincoln. (New York: Marion Mills Miller, ed., 1907).
4. Ex parte Merryman, 17 F. Cas. 144 (No. 9487) (C.C.D. Mo. 1861). From: Rehnquist, William. Civil Liberty and the Civil War. (Washington: The National Legal Center for the Public Interest, 1997.) 33-47.
5. *Id.* at 34.
6. President Lincoln's July 4, 1861 Message to Congress in Special Session. From: Messages and Papers of the Presidents, (Washington, D.C.: Bureau of National Literature, 1897), Vol. 7, p. 3227.
7. President Lincoln's July 4, 1861 Message to Congress in Special Session. From: Messages and Papers of the Presidents, (Washington D.C.: Bureau of National Literature, 1897), Vol. 7, p. 3227.
8. Opinion of Attorney General Edward Bates to President Lincoln regarding suspension of the privilege of the Writ of Habeas Corpus. July 5, 1861. From: Rehnquist, William. Civil Liberty and the Civil War. (Washington: The National Legal Center for the Public Interest, 1997.) 51.

9. Opinion of Attorney General Edward Bates to President Lincoln regarding suspension of the privilege of the Writ of Habeas Corpus. July 5, 1861. From: Rehnquist, William. Civil Liberty and the Civil War. (Washington: The National Legal Center for the Public Interest, 1997.) 52-53.

10. *Id.* at 53.

11. Opinion of Attorney General Edward Bates to President Lincoln regarding suspension of the privilege of the Writ of Habeas Corpus. July 5, 1861. From: Rehnquist, William. Civil Liberty and the Civil War. (Washington: The National Legal Center for the Public Interest, 1997.) 53.

12. Article 3, Section 2 of the U.S. Constitution.

13. Opinion of Attorney General Edward Bates to President Lincoln regarding suspension of the privilege of the Writ of Habeas Corpus. July 5, 1861. From: Rehnquist, William. Civil Liberty and the Civil War. (Washington: The National Legal Center for the Public Interest, 1997.) 54.

14. Ex parte Merryman, 17 F. Cas. 144 (No. 9487) (C.C.D. Mo. 1861).

15. Opinion of Attorney General Edward Bates to President Lincoln regarding suspension of the privilege of the Writ of Habeas Corpus. July 5, 1861. From: Rehnquist, William. Civil Liberty and the Civil War. (Washington: The National Legal Center for the Public Interest, 1997.) 56.

16. An Act to prevent settlements being made on lands ceded to the United States, until authorized by law, Statute II. Ninth Congress. Sess.II. Ch. 46. Mar. 3, 1807.

17. Opinion of Attorney General Edward Bates to President Lincoln regarding suspension of the privilege of the Writ of Habeas Corpus. July 5, 1861. From: Rehnquist, William. Civil Liberty and the Civil War. (Washington: The National Legal Center for the Public Interest, 1997.) 56-57.

18. Saldin, Robert P. Executive Power and the Constitution in Times of Crisis. White House Studies. 2004.

19. Kallenbach, Joseph. The American Chief Executive: The Presidency and the Governorship (New York: Harper and Row, 1966) 533.

20. Opinion of Attorney General Edward Bates to President Lincoln regarding suspension of the privilege of the Writ of Habeas Corpus. July 5, 1861. From: Rehnquist, William. Civil Liberty and the Civil War. (Washington: The National Legal Center for the Public Interest, 1997.) 57.

21. Justice Robert H. Jackson, dissenting opinion in Terminiello v. Chicago, 337 U.S. 1, 37, (1949).
22. Opinion of Attorney General Edward Bates to President Lincoln regarding suspension of the privilege of the Writ of Habeas Corpus. July 5, 1861. From: Rehnquist, William. Civil Liberty and the Civil War. (Washington: The National Legal Center for the Public Interest, 1997.) 58.
23. *Id.* at 58.
24. *Id.* at 59-60.
25. Opinion of Attorney General Edward Bates to President Lincoln regarding suspension of the privilege of the Writ of Habeas Corpus. July 5, 1861. From: Rehnquist, William. Civil Liberty and the Civil War. (Washington: The National Legal Center for the Public Interest, 1997.) 61-62.
26. *Id.* at 61-62.
27. Id. at 61.
28. Opinion of Attorney General Edward Bates to President Lincoln regarding suspension of the privilege of the Writ of Habeas Corpus. July 5, 1861. From: Rehnquist, William. Civil Liberty and the Civil War. (Washington: The National Legal Center for the Public Interest, 1997.) 62.
29. Id. at 62.
30. Id. at 62.
31. Opinion of Attorney General Edward Bates to President Lincoln regarding suspension of the privilege of the Writ of Habeas Corpus. July 5, 1861. From: Rehnquist, William. Civil Liberty and the Civil War. (Washington: The National Legal Center for the Public Interest, 1997.) 63.
32. Ex parte Merryman, 17 F. Cas. 144, 147 (No. 9487) (C.C.D. Mo. 1861).
33. *Id.* at 147.
34. *Id.* at 147.
35. *Id.* at 147.
36. Ex parte Merryman, 17 F. Cas. 144, 148 (No. 9487) (C.C.D. Mo. 1861).
37. *Id.* at 148.
38. *Id.* at 148.
39. Ex parte Merryman, 17 F. Cas. 144, 148 (No. 9487) (C.C.D. Mo. 1861).
40. *Id.* at 148.

41. *Id.* at 148.
42. Biographical Data of the U.S Congress - *http://bioguide.congress.gov/biosearch/biosearch1.asp* (showing that Congress was overwhelmingly Republican.)
43. An Act Relating to Habeas Corpus, And Regulating Judicial Proceedings In Certain Cases, 12 Stat. 755, March 3, 1863.
44. Justice Wayne, quoted in Washington Daily National Intelligencer, Sep. 18, 1861, p. 3. From: Silver, David. Lincoln's Supreme Court. (Urbana: University of Illinois Press, 1956.) p. 17.
45. Lincoln Fiction and Fact: An Interview with William Safire by Arthur Schlesinger. American Heritage Magazine, December 1987.
46. Executive usurpation [microform]: Speech of Hon. James A. Bayard, of Delaware, in the Senate of the United States, July 19, 1861.
47. Donald, David Herbert. Lincoln (New York: Touchstone, 1995) 305.
48. Ex parte Merryman, 17 F. Cas. 144, 149 (No. 9487) (C.C.D. Mo. 1861).
49. *Id.* at 149.
50. Ex parte Merryman, 17 F. Cas. 144, 149 (No. 9487) (C.C.D. Mo. 1861).
51. *Id.* at 149.
52. Justice Joseph Story. Commentaries on the Constitution 3. 1833. Vol. 3, Article 1, Section 9, Clause 2, Document 16. § 1336.
53. Ex parte Merryman, 17 F. Cas. 144 (No. 9487) (C.C.D. Mo. 1861).
54. Presidential Proclamation Suspending the Writ of Habeas Corpus Because of Resistance to the Draft, September 24, 1862. From: From: Rehnquist, William. Civil Liberty and the Civil War. (Washington: The National Legal Center for the Public Interest, 1997.) 67.
55. Presidential Proclamation Suspending the Writ of Habeas Corpus Because of Resistance to the Draft, September 24, 1862. From: Rehnquist, William. Civil Liberty and the Civil War. (Washington: The National Legal Center for the Public Interest, 1997.) 67.
56. An Act Relating to Habeas Corpus, And Regulating Judicial Proceedings In Certain Cases, 12 Stat. 755, March 3, 1863.
57. Robinson, William. Justice in Grey: A History of the Judicial System of the Confederate States of America. (Holmes Beach: W.M. W. Gaunt & Sons, Inc.) 383.
58. *Id.* at 383.
59. Confederate States of America Constitution.
60. Robinson, Justice in Grey 384-85.

61. *Id.* at 385-86.

62. *Id.* at 386.

63. Inglis v. The Sailor's Snug Harbor, 28 U.S. (3 Peters) 99 (1830), cited and discussed in the Daily Register (Knoxville), July 7, 1862.

64. The War of the Rebellion: A Compilation of the Official Records of the Union and Confederate Armies. Washington: Government Printing Office, 1880-1901. 2 series. II: 1373-1374.

65. *Id.* 1390-1394.

66. The War of the Rebellion: A Compilation of the Official Records of the Union and Confederate Armies. Washington: Government Printing Office, 1880-1901. 2 ser. II: 1390-1394.

67. *Id.* at 1393-1394.

68. Robinson, William. Justice in Grey: A History of the Judicial System of the Confederate States of America. (Holmes Beach: WM. W. Gaunt & Sons, Inc.) 390-91.

69. *Journal of the Congress of the Confederate States of America*, 1861-1865. Washington: Government Printing Office, 1904-1905. Vol. 2, 28-29, and v: 34; Stat. 1, I sess. C. 2 (Feb 27, 1862.)

70. *Id.* at 29.

71. *Journal of the Congress of the Confederate States of America*, 1861-1865. Washington: Government Printing Office, 1904-1905. Vol. 5, 130.

72. *Journal of the Congress of the Confederate States of America*, 1861-1865. Washington: Government Printing Office, 1904-1905. Vol. 5, 130.

73. *Id.* at Vol. 5, 235.

74. *Id.* at Vol. 5: 508-511, 516-518.

75. *Id* at. Vol. 6: 516.

76. *Id.* at Vol. 6: 517.

77. Opinions of the Confederate Attorney Generals: Writ of Habeas Corpus, Department of Justice, Richmond, VA, August 8, 1863. Letter from Att. Gen. T.H. Watts to President Jefferson Davis.

78. *Journal of the Congress of the Confederate States of America*, 1861-1865. Washington: Government Printing Office, 1904-1905. Vol. 3, 669-671, Vol. 6, 744-746.

79. *Journal of the Congress of the Confederate States of America*, 1861-1865. Washington: Government Printing Office, 1904-1905. Vol. 3: 669-671, Vol. 6, 744-746.

80. *Journal of the Congress of the Confederate States of America*, 1861-1865. Washington: Government Printing Office, 1904-1905. Vol. 3: 669-671, Vol. 6, 744-746.

81. Confederate Habeas Corpus Act, February 11, 1864. From: Confederate States of America Documents, Confederate Imprints: A Bibliography. (Austin: Jenkins Publishing Co.) 10.
82. Robinson, William. Justice in Grey: A History of the Judicial System of the Confederate States of America. (Holmes Beach: WM. W. Gaunt & Sons, Inc.) 408.
83. Robinson, William. Justice in Grey: A History of the Judicial System of the Confederate States of America. (Holmes Beach: WM. W. Gaunt & Sons, Inc.) 410.
84. Confederate Habeas Corpus Act, February 11, 1864. From: Confederate States of America Documents, Confederate Imprints: A Bibliography. (Austin: Jenkins Publishing Co.) 10.
85. *Id.* at 10.
86. Augusta Daily Chronicle & Sentinel, March 19 and April 3, 1864.
87. The Great Speech of Hon. A. H. Stephens, delivered before the Georgia Legislature, On Wednesday Night, March 16th, 1864. From: Morawski, Lee and Smith, Natalia. Documenting the South. (Chapel Hill: Apex Data Services, Inc.) 30.
88. The Great Speech of Hon. A. H. Stephens, delivered before the Georgia Legislature, On Wednesday Night, March 16th, 1864. From: Morawski, Lee and Smith, Natalia. Documenting the South. (Chapel Hill: Apex Data Services, Inc.) 29.
89. *Id.* at 29.
90. *Id.* at 30.
91. *Id.* at 30.
92. The Great Speech of Hon. A. H. Stephens, delivered before the Georgia Legislature, On Wednesday Night, March 16th, 1864. From: Morawski, Lee and Smith, Natalia. Documenting the South. (Chapel Hill: Apex Data Services, Inc.) 30.
93. *Id.* at 30.
94. *Id.* at 30.
95. *Id.* at 31.
96. *Id.* at 32.
97. Robinson, William. Justice in Grey: A History of the Judicial System of the Confederate States of America. (Holmes Beach: WM. W. Gaunt & Sons, Inc.) 412-14.
98. *Journal of the Congress of the Confederate States of America*, 1861-1865. Washington: Government Printing Office, 1904-1905. Vol. 7, 80-81.
99. *Id.* at 81.

The Myth and Reality of Legal Education in India

R. P. UPADHYAYA*

INTRODUCTION

THE importance and quality of Legal Education in democracy like ours is bound to affect the quality of judicial process, legal profession and administration of Law at all levels. So it has assumed status of National debate for its improvement in the Globalised situation. Among the various purposes, the legal education are obliged to serve the society by fostering skills with respect to Advocacy, Judicial Services and Law reforms. In fact Legal Education owes its existence to the overbearing needs of all Social, Economic, Political and Humanitarian considerations experienced by human civilization.

The objective requirement of Legal education are:

(i) To advance learning and knowledge of Law and Legal process.

(ii) To make the Legal processes efficient instrument of Social development.

(iii) The University and colleges shall be open to all persons of all religions of either sex irrespective of race, creed caste or class;

(iv) To develop in the students and research scholars a sense of responsibility to serve the society.

* *Principal in charge, Sikkim Government Law College, Sikkim.*

The main objective of Legal education were better explained by "*Lord Denning* in his address to the society of Public Teachers of Law. He emphasized three purposes of Legal education[1].

(a) How legal rules have developed.

(b) How nexus between Legal and Social history have been established.

(c) To show the right path to the society for further development in view of Justice.

Historical Development of Legal Education in India

Before - coming to the central point of discussion on the topic I want to throw a few light on historical development of legal education in India specially after independence.

The legal profession in India was recognized by Lord-Cornwall is in 1793 for the first time during British regime. Gradually it was developed in different universities of India with different syllabus. After independence of India, the Parliament by enacting Advocate Act 1961 has given autonomy to the Bar council of India on Legal education. Beside it other autonomous bodies like university grant commission, ministry of Higher education and Ministry of Law & Justice and university and Colleges are other segment of control over Legal education including Central Government, which has abolished apprenticeship system of Examination in early 1960's. Before introducing 3 years course in 1967, two years course was in existence. For entry to the Legal profession, the Bar council was holding the examinations under the provisions of section 28(2) read with section 24(i)(d) of the Advocate Act. However, the training and examinations were abolished by the central Government in exercise of powers under section 49-A. The Central Government again under 49-A framed the rules called Advocate(Right to take up Teaching) Rules 1979, allowing the Advocates while practicing to take up teaching of Law, so long as the hours during which he is engaged in teaching of Law do not exceed three hours a day . it encouraged the commercialization of Legal education. In 1976 U.G.C appointed a joint consultative committee with Bar council education committee which recommended the practice of admitting graduate to LL.B Course and also recommended a four years integrated LL.B degree course after 10+2 to be tried in few selected universities. The recommendations were sent to the Bar Council and also circulated to the universities. On 29th August 1980, the university grants Commission agreed with the views of the Bar council to introduce a four years LL.B integrated course after 10+2 with regard to proposal of 2years after Graduation should be followed by an additional course of one year so that the course should be inconformity with 3 years of India LL.B degree course as recommended by the Bar Council of India for enrolment as an Advocate. On April 17,1982, Bar Council of India arranged a meeting of Legal Education committee with member of Law Panel of the University Grant Commission. The Committee unanimously decided that Law course should be of 5 years after 10+2 and it also include practical training as an essential part of professional education. In 1983, there was a conference of Vice-Chancellors of the University of U.P. opposing the implementation of 5 years Law Course. On 1st November 1983, UG.C issued a circular to the Universities for adopting 5 years integrated course after 10+2 in due course of time. On 25, 26, 1983, a workshop was held at Pune University and Maharastra Bar Council where 5 years Law Course was criticized among others by the then Chief Justice of India. Due to this reason, a pressure was created by Law Minister as well as Planning Minister on Bar Council of India to drop 5 years Course. In case it is not accepted, the central Government will make a rule under section 49-A superseding the effect of Bar council rule to implement 5 years Law course. In such circumstances, the Bar council of India adopted amid way by taking a decision to allow 5 years course & 3years Law Course simultaneously. The main reason for implementation of 5years Law course was that the most of Law Colleges of the Country were handled by part time Law teachers and the State or Central Government was also not ready to bear the extra burden. However, last few years, Law Minister, Judges & academicians while expressing concern in the fall of standard of Legal Education, have recommended 5 years Law Course.

The idea of establishing National Law Schools as autonomous Universities under respective State statute was born out of genuine need for improving the quality of Legal Education. The first National Law School of India University(NLSIU) -was set up by the Government of the Karnataka at Banglore in 1985, towards improving the quality of Legal Education. All India Law Ministers conference (1995) resolved to set up in each State a Law School Model on the line of the NISIU on the basis of recommendations made by the committee on Legal Education and training appointed by the Chief Justices conference in 1993.

The promoters of National Law University were determined to bring about perceptive changes in the quality of Legal Education in India to draw it at par with the world standards. The Programme, which was carefully drawn, has started to yield encouraging results where the Graduates of Indian NLU are increasingly being sought for both within the country and outside.

The number of NLU has already passed two decade and by end of the current plan period, it is likely to be double. This is a welcome move but there is an apprehension for generality and compromise of quality. Hence need has arisen to reformulate the conceptual intricacies existing in law schools to ensure of individual sustainability and collective progress in view emerging dimension of legal education in the world as well as by adopting co-ordinate approach on the other.

The cost of quality education is constantly on the rise. The traditional class room education has given way to webside browsing for updating information . building up of appropriate law library and other basic physical infrastructure of corresponding measure, involve huge investment. In order to secure all round development of law students, all the premier institutions have build up infrastructure for co-curricular and extra-curricular activities. There is a need for exchange programmes of the students and faculties.

How to Improve the Quality of Legal Education

The Bar council of India, National Law school and University have attempted a lot to improve the quality of legal education and to some extent they have improved the legal education in India to bring it at par with the world standard but still more is required to be done in due course of time which may be mentioned as follows-

(a) Admission of students in university or colleges.

(b) Infrastructure development

(c) Financial management (income & expenditure)

(d) Security to the poor and needy students

(e) Co-curricular & extracurricular activities.

(a) Admission of Students in the Universisty or Colleges: The admission system in NLUs has become a combined process through introduction of common law admission Test (CLAT). It provides for adequate reservation of schedule caste, schedule tribe and physically challenge persons . on the same pattern for admission in central university or state University or colleges, the Centre or State with assistance of University or college officers, admission test is to be conducted and as per requirement of University or colleges students should be send for admission in order of merit considering the reservation of S.C ST,O.B.C. or physically challenged persons. It will help in improvement or legal education.

(b) Infrastructure development: Construction of different class rooms, chambers for professors, building up an appropriate law library and other basic physical infrastructure of corresponding measure, involve huge investment. Their maintainance and up-gradation account for major share of revenue expenditure. It is to be developed and done by the Government by fixing responsibility upon some officer of the University or colleges at one time but regular expenditure of maintenance is to be maintained by the University or College it self.

(c) Financial Management: Financial management has two major segments- Income Management and expenditure management. The income management is oriented towards generation enough resource that can adequately support the expenditure needs. As the demands for expenditure grow , need for income augmentation grows. Government's Grant-in-aid have traditionally been accepted as the most important component of income, beside the imperativeness of the universities or colleges to become self supportive is live survival issue. The other sources of income are: (i) fees from students (ii) Donations and endowments (iii) Industry support (iv) Publication Royalties (v) Outreach programmes (vi) Sponsored Research studies and Training Programmes.

(c) The Important areas of expenditure management areas are:

(i) *Budget:* The expenditure budget must necessarily be drawn in a manner that can provide adequately for priority activities. It should be zero based and cover all foreseeable contingencies.

(ii) *Control Mechanism:* At the time of execution, the tenets prudent fiscal norms must be applied so that there is neither under spending nor overspending.

(iii) *Responsibility Centre:* Heads of the centres and colleges may be vested with appropriate financial and spending powers under well defined responsibility and accountability norms. This brings a healthy competition among the colleges to outperform and grow.

(d) Financial Security to the poor and needy students: Security to the poor and needy Students during the course of their studies may be ensured in following ways.

(i) Study loans from Bank (ii) Freeship and Scholarship (iii) Earn-as-you learn Scheme (iv) Sponsored projects (v) Seminar and workshop Assistance.

Some other short coming of Legal Education are as follows:

(a) Outdated method of teaching

(b) Lack of Research and development facility

(c) Faulty Regulation system

(d) Lack of proper Policy for financial

(e) Lack of proper University Industry interaction

(f) Inappropriate growth in number of Legal Education Students

Measusres to Resolve the problems in the Legal Educational System

(a) Upgradation of Curricular

(b) Productivity of Orientation

(c) Value Education

(d) Research

(e) Combination of Equity and excellance

(f) Incentive to open New Institutions

(g) Fee Structure should be revised

(h) Financial help to poor students

(i) Proper inspection before entry of foreign institutions

(j) Transparency

(k) Adopt the concept of Reciprocity

Some other Reasons for Improving Quality of Legal Education

The promises: Of late, Political Leaders at the helm have been taking initative an promising the public, the establishing a new universities even by starving the already existing ones of funds essential for their sound running and consolidation. In so promising and starting universities, they do little planning, except thinking of vote for the next election. This results in a burden of recurring financial obligations.

The Shackles: Writing on the quality of university education, pro. S.L.Sharma laid down five norms (a) Quality Syllabus, (b) Quality teaching and evaluation) (c) Quality research (d) Quality faculty (e) Quality Character[2].

The Quality: when we speak of quality faculty, a thorough overhauling of the policy, governing the selection of the faculty alongwith depth in the subject, the aspirant for entry into faculty has to possess the quality delivery as well. If the U.G.C. and NAAC go for a scanning of the existing faculties in the universities or colleges, they are sure to find at least fifty per cent of them needing corrective speech therapy, unclear voice, hasty delivery and quite often incomprehensive expression are their drawbacks.

The Apathy: Medium of instruction has become another detracting problem. Every state Government has its own agenda to promote its local language. Except the courses in language departments, all other courses depend on reference book in English, which are stacked in good numbers in University libraries .some of those , who have been raring to go for professorship and even some of those already professors, are unable to understand the contents of the books by standard authors.

The Dereliction: Faculty, getting into the groove under the umbrella of certain consideration like caste affinity an unfair means, can seldom deliver good. A university teacher with unteacher like qualities doing contracts outside, stayed away for years, but yet found a fevourable re-entry into university's pay rolls with the support of our unpredictable legal recourse and a fevouable state administration, draw arrears of his salary ,running into lakhs of rupees.

SUGGESTIONS

(a) The Indian Education system is generally marks based. However, some experiments have been made to do away with the marks based system which has led to cases of depression and suicide among students.

(b) Outdoor Education is relatively new to schools in India though it is quite well established abroad. Acceptance is slowly increasing in this regard with few schools, may also be considered by the Bar Council of India to some extent where it is possible.

(c) India has a large number of distance education programmes in undergraduate and Post graduate levels. Initially it was started by private Institutions. By 1985 many of the larger Universities recognized the need and potential of distance education. So if it is also taken into account by the Bar Council of India, will help to many poor students of rural areas in India.

(d) At present knowledge is turned into commodity. A marketable sample of special kind of knowledge is the currency of modern world. National Law Schools are model for market oriented education. So Bar Council of India should also try to take the matter from National Law School and include it in the curriculam of Law Schools of the College in India . Bar Council of India by it new rule 2008 had attempted to achieve some part but more is needed in this regard.

Notes

1. M. N. Mathur, 'Legal Education and Bar Council', *Indian Bar Review*, Vol. XXIV, (3&4), 1987.
2. *Universisty News*, 42-3:3

Index